MW01038727

SAVE THE PEOPLE!

SAVE THE PEOPLE!

HALTING HUMAN EXTINCTION

STACY McANULTY

WITH ART BY NICOLE MILES

LITTLE, BROWN AND COMPANY

New York Boston

Text copyright © 2022 by Stacy McAnulty
Illustrations copyright © 2022 by Nicole Miles

Cover art copyright © 2022 by Nicole Miles. Cover design by Jenny Kimura.
Cover copyright © 2022 by Hachette Book Group, Inc.

Cloud vector (as on page 5) © Ihor Biliavskyi/Shutterstock.com; splatter
background (as on page 5) © Golden Shrimp/Shutterstock.com; brush vectors (as on
page 165) © Olga_C/Shutterstock.com; rough edge vectors in sidebars © Ollie The
Designer/Shutterstock.com; grunge background in sidebars © ilolab/Shutterstock.com

Hachette Book Group supports the right to free expression and the value of copyright.
The purpose of copyright is to encourage writers and artists to produce the creative
works that enrich our culture.

The scanning, uploading, and distribution of this book without permission is a theft
of the author's intellectual property. If you would like permission to use material from
the book (other than for review purposes), please contact permissions@hbgusa.com.
Thank you for your support of the author's rights.

Little, Brown and Company
Hachette Book Group
1290 Avenue of the Americas, New York, NY 10104
Visit us at LBYR.com

First Edition: May 2022

Little, Brown and Company is a division of Hachette Book Group, Inc.
The Little, Brown name and logo are trademarks of Hachette Book Group, Inc.

The publisher is not responsible for websites (or their content)
that are not owned by the publisher.

Library of Congress Cataloging-in-Publication Data
Names: McAnulty, Stacy, author.
Title: Save the people! : halting human extinction / Stacy McAnulty.
Description: First edition. | New York : Little, Brown and Company, 2022. | Includes
bibliographical references and index. | Audience: Ages: 8–12 | Summary: "A book for
middle-school-aged children about previous extinctions and possible threats to humans,
from volcanoes, to asteroids, to pollution and diseases." —Provided by publisher.
Identifiers: LCCN 2021027527 | ISBN 9780759553941 (hardcover) |
ISBN 9780759553989 (ebook)
Subjects: LCSH: Extinction (Biology)—Juvenile literature. | Mass extinctions—
Juvenile literature. | Human beings—Effect of environment on—Juvenile literature. |
Human beings—Effect of climate on—Juvenile literature. | Nature—Effect of human
beings on—Juvenile literature. | Human beings—Extinction—Juvenile literature.
Classification: LCC QH78 .M325 2022 | DDC 576.84—dc23
LC record available at https://lccn.loc.gov/2021027527

ISBNs: 978-0-7595-5394-1 (hardcover), 978-0-7595-5398-9 (ebook)

Printed in the United States of America

LSC-C

Printing 1, 2022

FOR PAST STACY
(I'LL EXPLAIN IN THE ACKNOWLEDGMENTS.)

CONTENTS

PART III: WHAT'S GOING WRONG TODAY

DEAR POTENTIAL READER,

This book is not for everyone. That's a strange thing to admit when I'm hoping to sell a million copies. Because these chapters are bursting with scary but true information, some people—mainly adults, I imagine—will want to close the cover and ignore the *danger*s looming inside. But looking the other way doesn't make threats disappear. To come up with solutions, we must arm ourselves with knowledge and science. (You know *science*, the subject that brought us antibiotics, the internet, and the recipe for homemade slime.)

Save the People! Halting Human Extinction is what I'd call "nonfiction horror," which is probably not currently a section in your library or favorite bookstore. With the way things are going, though, maybe it will be soon. In these pages, we will examine frightening topics like mass extinction and the ~~in-evitable~~ *potential* demise of our planet. Some of these events have already occurred, others will probably never happen (thankfully), still others are possible, and one is well underway. (Spoiler alert: It's climate change.)

If you don't like scary stories, you might be tempted to put this book down. No hard feelings. However, if you believe in the power of science and humans' problem-solving abilities, *and* you're brave enough to confront perilous possibilities, I encourage you to soldier forward. Grab a flashlight and a friend (that's how I like to watch horror movies), and get ready to take a scientific journey from Earth's past through today and beyond, to our questionable future. Who knows? Someday, you may hold the key to saving the people.

All my best,

Stacy

PART I

IN THE BEGINNING

LET'S FIRST LEARN FROM THE PAST

"Those who fail to learn from history are condemned to re-peat it," British prime minister Winston Churchill said in 1948, borrowing from philosopher George Santayana. Chur-chill probably wasn't referring to the birth of our solar sys-tem or the extinction of dinosaurs, but knowing our science history is essential to understanding today's world and to-day's threats.

So let's jump into the past and see where we came from before we look at where we're heading. With any luck, we won't repeat what the dinosaurs lived through.

…Actually, they didn't live through it.

CHAPTER 1

EARTH

A VERY BRIEF HISTORY

Buckle up! This is going to be a ridiculously quick ride through time and space, so keep your arms and legs inside the vehicle at all times. If you have questions, don't worry. We'll take a deeper dive into the most intense ideas once we catch our breaths.

13.8 BILLION YEARS AGO

CONGRATULATIONS! IT'S A UNIVERSE!

Once upon a time, our universe began with a bang. A big one! Originally, the universe was smaller than the period at the end of this sentence, and then energy, matter, and time were created in a blink.

13.7 BILLION YEARS AGO

STAR LIGHT, STAR BRIGHT, FIRST STAR I SEE TONIGHT...

About 180 million years after the big bang, the universe got its first stars.

4.6 BILLION YEARS AGO

CONGRATULATIONS! IT'S A SUN!

Our neighborhood star is obviously our favorite (don't tell the others), and it came on the scene a whopping 9 billion years after those first stars. Before the sun became *the* sun, it was an enormous rotating ball of dust and gas, AKA a nebula.

A PLACE TO CALL HOME.

The leftover dust and gas that didn't join the burning hot sun became our solar system—a collection of eight planets (which does not include Pluto), at least five dwarf planets (which *does* include Pluto), over 150 moons, thousands of comets, and millions of asteroids.

CONGRATULATIONS! IT'S A MOON!

Earth's first years were lifeless and harsh. Especially one day during the Late Heavy Bombardment period, when a Mars-sized rock crashed into Earth. Scientists call this boulder Theia. On impact, Theia was obliterated, and so was a portion of Earth. This crash shot debris thousands of miles into space, but over time, Earth's gravity captured some of these chunks and wrapped them into a neat little ball. And thus, our moon was born. So basically, the moon is Earth and Theia's child.

THEIA

EARTH

4.5 BILLION-ISH YEARS AGO

SPLISH, SPLASH!

Earth continued to be pelted with space rocks and experienced very violent volcanic activity. Then things cooled off and got wet. About 100 million years after Theia's impact, water covered nearly the entire planet. Some small islands may have dotted the waterscape, but Earth was definitely in its bluest-of-blue phase. Most of our planet's surface water probably came from magma cooling (picture steam escaping as molten rock solidified). Some H_2O may have been delivered from outer space via icy comets.

OVER THE NEXT BILLION YEARS

LAND AHOY!

Large proto-continents (meaning: early continents) slowly appeared. Earth was no longer just H_2O on the surface, but the land was barren and boring. The seas weren't exactly exciting either, though scientists have discovered fossils from simple microscopic life that existed 3.5 billion years ago. (Sadly, no one was around to jot down the exact date life began on Earth. Go figure.)

2.7 BILLION YEARS AGO

JUST BREATHE.

Finally, oxygen! Pro tip: If you ever time travel, be sure not to go back further than 2.7 billion years. Or, if you do, wear a space suit with an oxygen tank. For its first 1.8 billion years, our planet lacked this gas.

1.85 BILLION- 850 MILLION YEARS AGO

YAWN.

Geologists call this time frame the Boring Billion because Earth didn't change much. I'm not going to argue with these scientists. Let's move on.

579 MILLION YEARS AGO

TIME TO PRESS DEFROST.

In the millennia (meaning: thousands of years) before this time, our planet had been in its Snowball Earth phase. Ice covered the globe from the poles to the equator. This is also known as the Big Brrr! (Okay, I'm the only one who calls it that.) Ice ages happened repeatedly in Earth's history. But after this particular cold spell, life (finally!) got a kick start.

541 MILLION- 530 MILLION YEARS AGO

BOOM! AN EXPLOSION.

Things got exciting with the Cambrian explosion (no TNT required!). We're talking about a sudden boom in life-forms! This all took place in shallow seas that covered the planet. What little dry land existed was still barren—no trees, no shrubs, no bugs, no plants, no Starbucks. Before the Cambrian explosion, life-forms munched on chemicals and absorbed energy, like sunlight. Now Earth had creatures that could move around and eat other creatures. *Yum!*

444 MILLION YEARS AGO

BUH-BYE!

Critters of this era experienced Earth's first mass extinction. Turns out, this will be a common cycle for Earth—new life-forms flourish, then a mass extinction presses the reset button. The planet has experienced this five times since the Cambrian explosion, and signs point to a sixth mass extinction ringing the bell from our doorstep.

(Stay tuned: much more on mass extinctions in Chapters 2 and 3.)

383 MILLION-359 MILLION YEARS AGO	*TAKE TWO.* Another mass extinction.
252 MILLION YEARS AGO	*TAKE THREE.* Another mass extinction. This one is known as the Great Dying. Because "great" is in the title, we know it's got to be awesome.
230 MILLION YEARS AGO	*HELLO, SLOW, NOT-SO-SMART DINOSAURS.* The first dinosaurs scampered across the planet. But don't imagine *Jurassic Park*–type reptiles. These dinos were small, but the start of something big.
201 MILLION YEARS AGO	*TAKE FOUR.* Another mass extinction.
66 MILLION YEARS AGO	*TAKE FIVE.* Another mass extinction. This one wiped out the dinosaurs. (Stay tuned: much more on dinosaurs in Chapter 3.)
2.5 MILLION YEARS AGO	*MEET OUR NOT-SO-DISTANT COUSINS.* Let's selfishly fast-forward to *human* times. *Homo erectus* (translation: upright man) was one of the earliest human species, and the first to pack their bags and venture out of Africa—walking on two feet, of course. They survived for 2 million years on this planet, which is about ten times longer than our current reign. (Stay tuned: much more on humans in Chapter 4.)

300,000 YEARS AGO

HOMO SAPIENS! AKA: US!

Your great-great-great-great-great-great-...grand-parents started roaming the planet. Scientifically speaking, this wasn't that long ago! Imagine all of Earth's 4.54 billion years condensed into a seven-hour school day with the planet's formation happening just as the first bell rang. *Homo sapiens* would not join the class until there was about one second left in the day. We are a relatively new, invasive species in this world. We are everywhere. We are multiplying. We are taking over—it's safe to call us an aggressive organism.

12,000 YEARS AGO

HUMANS SETTLE DOWN AND PLANT SOME ROOTS.

We *Homo sapiens* think we're pretty sophisticated with our upright posture, big brains, and smartphones. But most of our time as a species has been spent as potential prey, not as dominant predators. (Though we've probably always fought *each other* for resources.) Until 12,000 years ago, we made our living hunting and gathering, with an emphasis on gathering. Then we turned to farming, which allowed us to settle down, produce more food, and advance our societies. But farming is backbreaking hard work and probably had some folks wishing for the good ole days of berry picking and mastodon hunting.

(Stay tuned: much more on the rise of *Homo sapiens* in Chapter 5.)

580 YEARS AGO

MORE BOOKS ARE POSSIBLE!

Johannes Gutenberg invented the printing press in Europe, an important development for bookmaking (and education and communication). *Thank you, Mr. Gutenberg!* Though Pi Sheng created movable type in China about four hundred years earlier. *Thank you, Mr. Sheng!*

250 YEARS AGO

GETTING INDUSTRIOUS.

The first industrial revolution began in a small corner of the world called England. Technological and scientific advancements moved workers from the fields and cottages to the factories and offices. Coal (a fossil fuel) became a popular option for heating homes, powering trains and ships, and manufacturing iron, steel, and other materials.

150 YEARS AGO

GETTING INDUSTRIOUS, TAKE TWO.

The second industrial revolution took off, and so did our devotion to fossil fuels, *which* put carbon in the atmosphere, *which* has affected our planet's temperature, *which* may spell disaster for future humans.

(Stay tuned: much more on our love of and dependency on energy in Part III.)

75 YEARS AGO

NUKED!

Humans made the first nuclear bomb. Sadly, wars are nothing new to us, and battles even predate written history. But the invention of the atomic bomb suddenly made our species very efficient at killing one another.

(Stay tuned: much more on warring and nukes in Chapter 10.)

50 YEARS AGO

ONE GIANT LEAP FOR MANKIND.

On July 20, 1969, astronauts walked on the moon—the first non-Earth place humans visited. But decades later, the moon is still not an earthling vacation destination. NASA hopes to send astronauts (and not just male astronauts) back to the moon in the 2020s and also wants to explore Mars up close and in person in the 2030s, though the 2040s might be more likely.

YESTERDAY ○ *JUST ONE DAY AGO.*

You should really remember what happened yesterday.

TODAY ○ *YOUR HOME.*

Earth is home to about 7.9 billion *Homo sapiens* and millions of species of plants and animals. Earth's flora and fauna live on land, in water, in ice caps, near undersea volcanoes, and on international space stations. Earth is a unique planet (at least in our solar system) capable of hosting a multitude of life. Some of it is even intelligent life, like you, me, and labrador retrievers.

TOMORROW ○ *WHAT DOES THE CRYSTAL BALL SAY?*

Earth has ideal conditions for us to eat, sleep, breathe, and play *Minecraft*, but is this optimal environment going to stick around? We certainly want the answer to be "Oh, yeah!"

In the next chapters, we'll take a closer look at the history of Earth's catastrophes and the numerous potential threats to our planet. But let's be honest: Earth can withstand just about anything (except what's in Chapter 11). It's us humans—the delicate beings we are—who require a specific environment with particular ingredients. And it's up to us to understand (and hopefully save) this planet for our own sake.

WHERE WE HANG

Let's discuss your address. It contains a
street, a city or town, a state, a country, and
a galaxy. Our little turf exists in the Milky
Way galaxy—which was named *before* the
candy bar. It comes from the Latin *via lac-
tea*, which translates as "the road of milk"
or "Milky Avenue" or "Milky Way." (Check
out the night sky. Does it look like splattered
milk?) Specifically, we are in the Orion Spur
of the Milky Way. We reside in *our* solar system. Like *our* sun and *our* moon, *our* solar
system doesn't get a unique name. Just *our*
solar system. And we all live on planet Earth.
From here, our addresses will vary, but every
reader of this book is a land-dwelling mammal (even if you live on a boat), with at least
99.9 percent of your DNA matching every
other person on the planet. *We're all neighbors! We're all family!*

SUN

MERCURY

VENUS

EARTH!

MARS

JUPITER

SATURN

URANUS

NEPTUNE

CHAPTER 2

MASS EXTINCTIONS

THE FIRST FOUR OF FIVE

TIME FOR SCARY STORIES

Mass extinction: an event when at least 75 percent of all species are terminated. *Poof!* These are the horror stories of Earth's natural past. Like any terrifying tales, they're fun to hear about, but it would stink to participate in them. Scientists have identified five big ones over the past half billion years:

- Ordovician-Silurian extinction
  - 444 million years ago (mya)
  - 85% of species croaked

- Devonian extinction
  - 383 mya–359 mya
  - 70–80% of all animal species perished

- Permian extinction, or the Great Dying
  - 252 mya
  - 95% of marine species and 70% of land species permanently checked out

- End-Triassic extinction
  - 201 mya
  - 76% of species kicked the bucket
- Cretaceous-Tertiary extinction
  - 66 mya
  - 80% of animal species died, including all non-avian dinosaurs

While these are the big, known events, mass extinctions also occurred before 450 million years ago, like when oxygen came along and all the organisms that didn't like this new gas died. But the life-forms of a half billion years ago were microscopic, and the fossil evidence needed to study these ancient events is hard to obtain. (But not impossible! They're called microfossils.)

DIG IT! FOSSILS!

Fossils are time capsules of plants or animals recorded in rock. These can be preserved remnants of the organism (like dinosaur bones) or preserved traces of the organism (like dinosaur footprints). Fossils are ancient, usually at least 10,000 years old, and they are the best records of the history of life on Earth. Unfortunately, fossils represent

only a tiny fraction of all old-timey organisms because the circumstances need to be ideal for their creation. For example, a dead woolly rhino needs to be quickly buried in mud or ash before scavengers turn the beast into a buffet. Then the carcass needs to be undisturbed for thousands of years as the mud turns to rock under geological pressure. Fossil records also tend to favor hard materials such as bones, horns, and shells. We have less ancient evidence of soft stuff.

Let's look at the first four mass extinctions here. (The dinosaur extinction, which we could argue is the most infamous, will be covered in Chapter 3.)

ORDOVICIAN-SILURIAN EXTINCTION

AKA: End-Ordovician Extinction (because, well, the Ordovician era ended)

Rank: Silver Medal! The Second Worst

What Life Looked Like Before:

If we could travel back 460 million years, we'd find a round and wet Earth, and we wouldn't recognize much else. This is the time of the "sea without fish," though that's not entirely accurate. Proto-fish (meaning: early fish) swam about, but they didn't look like trout, bass, tuna, or anything we might catch with a rod and reel today. And they were *rare*. Instead, alien-looking invertebrates (meaning: spineless creatures) dominated the seas. They crept and crawled along the floor of an underwater world.

Earth's sea levels were at their highest. It was a warm and wet world with very little ice, even at the poles. Life flourished almost solely in the water, either in the vast ocean or the shallow seas across the continents. Even places we now know as Wisconsin and Siberia were covered in knee-high water. Some plants, like liverwort, may have nestled near the water's edge, but what little dry land existed was barren.

If we could view this ancient world from space, we'd see

that it was bottom heavy. All the landmasses (which, again, were mostly covered in shallow seas) hung out in the southern hemisphere. The king of the continents was Gondwana, which consisted basically of modern-day Africa, South America, Antarctica, and Australia mashed together. North America was part of the continent of Laurentia. The Panthalassic Ocean dominated the northern half of the globe.

And the differences to the modern world continue. The sun was 3 to 5 percent less bright. Earth rotated faster, with a day lasting about twenty hours. The air had more carbon dioxide (CO_2) and less oxygen (O_2), hence the balmy temperatures. There was no Wi-Fi.

SCIENTIFIC THEORIES

Pause. Let's stop for a moment and note that the reasons for mass extinctions are never simple, and they're often debated. As technology advances, scientists can learn more about the past and create new, better theories about long-ago destruction. But until someone invents a time machine, humans will continue to debate any event from the BCC era. (BCC? That's my acronym for the Before Cell-Phone Cameras era.) *Unpause.*

What Likely Happened:

The last centuries of the Ordovician burst with excitement: major volcanic activity and asteroid strikes. Yet these events likely didn't cause our first mass extinction. The popular theory for the loss of 85 percent of Earth's species is the dawn of an ice age. *Climate change!* Gondwana drifted to the South Pole and became a hot spot for glaciers (well, maybe "hot" is the wrong word). More and more glaciers formed, trapping water and drying shallow seas across the early continents. Suddenly, real estate became a problem, and the water-dwelling critters were homeless.

Also, the new Appalachian mountain range formed, which led to carbon dioxide being sucked out of the air. We think of trees as CO_2 gobblers with their awesome photosynthesis skills, but rock erosion also nibbles away at the gas. (Recipe: Take rocks loaded with calcium and magnesium, add CO_2 captured in rainwater, and combine to create limestone.)

The general rule: The more CO_2 in the atmosphere, the warmer Earth's temperature. Less CO_2 means a cooler planet. (Trust me, we'll hear this a lot.)

When the Ordovician era's warm-and-wet-loving creatures were thrown into a cold and dry environment, the result was apocalyptic.

Famous Victims:

- Some species of brachiopods. They look like clams, but they're not.
- Some species of conodonts. They look like eels, but they're not.
- Some species of trilobites. They have exoskeletons like insects and lobsters, but they're not. *Isotelus rex*—the world's largest trilobite ever—went buh-bye forever. One fossilized *I. rex* was over 2.3 feet long.

This extinction took out plenty of species but not entire taxonomic families. (It would be like if the giant panda went extinct, not all bears would be extinct. We'd still have polar bears, brown bears, etc.) Think of it like trimming the tree of life but not cutting off entire branches. This is a good thing. Because new species can rise up after things calm down.

DEVONIAN EXTINCTION

AKA: Late Devonian Extinction
Rank: The Fifth and Least Impressive (or is it?)

What Life Looked Like Before:

Now we travel from the "sea without fish" (though technically not accurate) to the Age of Fishes in the Devonian period. Some of these critters appeared more fishlike, but some certainly did not. Like placoderms: terrifying, armored fish that would keep me from going even knee-deep in the water. The king of these beasts was *Dunkleosteus*, which could grow to thirty feet long. That's the size of a school bus! A third of its body size was an armored head. Dunks didn't have teeth but instead had self-sharpening blades. Its bite force is considered the strongest of any fish *ever* and could rival that of a *T. rex*. And because *Dunkleosteus* could open its bottom *and* top jaw (humans, sharks, and most other animals move only their bottom jaw), it created a suction that inhaled its prey. *Dunkleosteus* had no predators to worry about, except other *Dunkleosteus*. Maybe they fought over territory, or maybe they ate each other. It's hard to say. But fossil evidence shows they definitely had cage matches, just without the cages.

Armored predators and other vicious swimmers made the seas terrifying. Maybe that's why some fish crept out of the water. For the first time, the world became a home for tetrapods—animals with vertebrae (meaning: spines or backbones) and four limbs that live on land. (Hey, we're tetrapods. *Go, team tetrapods!*) Also, the land wasn't plant-free anymore. By the mid-Devonian, Earth had proto-trees (meaning: early trees), which were more like thirty-foot-tall weeds. Later came a 100-foot-tall tree called *Archaeopteris* that had a root system. Still, overall, the seas were more diverse and lively than the land.

What Likely Happened:

This was a long, deadly event. The Devonian extinction lasted 20 million to 25 million years and had at least two peaks (and perhaps a few smaller extinction blips): The Kellwasser Event happened 374 million years ago, and the Hangenberg Event 359 million years ago. During the Kellwasser Event, over 3 million square miles of the world's reefs died off. The reason for this extinction episode is unknown. (Or at least scientists are nowhere near an agreement yet.)

The second punch resulted in an ice age, which lasted 100 million years and is the longest ice age of the past billion years. *Climate change!* The cause of this big chill required teamwork. Trees—doing what trees do—sucked CO_2 out of the air and caused temperatures to drop. (The less CO_2 in the atmosphere, the lower the global temperature.) Rain runoff deposited sediment from all these new trees, plants, and soil into the seas, which messed up the water's chemical balance. Volcanic activity also poisoned the oceans. (Volcanoes are frequent villains in mass extinctions.) Glaciers moved in and froze both fresh and salty H_2O, destroying habitats. Earth became a planet only Elsa could love.

CO₂ IN   O₂ OUT

Famous Victims:

- Our scary friend *Dunkleosteus*.
- More species of trilobites but not all. They're hanging in there.
- Some species of coral.

PERMIAN EXTINCTION

AKA: The Great Dying
Rank: *We're Number One! We're Number One!*

What Life Looked Like Before:

Finally! Things were *really* happening on land. After Earth's longest ice age of the animal era, giant critters existed outside the seas. Massive herbivores and carnivores roamed, including the 11.5-foot-long *Dimetrodon*. This spiny animal is often mistaken for a dinosaur. It's not. Dinosaurs were still millions of years in the future, and *Dimetrodon* was more closely related to mammals.

This was also the time of Pangea, the single giant landmass that ran from the Arctic to the Antarctic. And a single ocean called Panthalassa. Trees and weeds covered the landscape, but no grasses or flowers yet. Earth was also swarming with insects. *Bzzzzzz.*

What Likely Happened:

The greatest mass extinction in Earth's history was

primarily thanks to volcanoes in Russia known as the Siberian Traps. These are not your typical volcanoes that you model in your kitchen with baking soda and vinegar. The Siberian Trap eruptions were massive, producing enough lava to cover an area the size of the continental United States a half mile deep. But the lava caused only localized damage. While the CO_2 it spit into the air cooked the entire planet. Heat waves across Pangea could have reached 140°F (60°C). *Climate change!* (Friendly reminder for a third time: A rise in CO_2 means a rise in temperature.) The world became a hothouse, and the proto-mammals (meaning: early mammals) that lived on land suffered. Trees essentially disappeared. And this is the only mass extinction that wiped out a ton of insects. Bugs are usually troopers during mass extinctions. Not this time.

Things weren't better in the seas. The ocean warmed and acidified. Not good! A warmer ocean holds less oxygen, and an acidic ocean is a big-time killer for reefs and any critter with a shell. (Remember this fact for when we get to Part III.) Earth nearly became uninhabitable. Yep, this was the closest the planet has come to a complete wipeout.

Famous Victims:

- The rest of the placoderms, those armored fish.
- A mammal-like reptile called *Moschops*.
- The largest insect ever, *Meganeuropsis*.

- Our not-a-dino friend *Dimetrodon*.
- The rest of the trilobites, which had survived the other two mass extinctions.

This extinction was the big one! Earth nearly became like all the other planets in our solar system—lifeless! It's estimated that 95 percent of all marine species and 70 percent of land species died off. The Permian extinction didn't just trim the tree of life; it butchered branches. Half of all taxonomic families vanished.

END-TRIASSIC EXTINCTION

AKA: Triassic Extinction, Triassic-Jurassic Extinction, Not-the-Dinosaur Extinction
Rank: Number Four

What Life Looked Like Before:

Recovering from the Great Dying took a while. Trees missed out on the first 10 million years of the period, but plant life—and animals too—eventually rebounded. The Early Triassic climate was hot, and critters preferred to hang out near the poles, avoiding the intense heat around the equator. This is the age of the reptiles, when croc-like beings dominated. These beasts didn't resemble the low-to-the-ground, four-legged reptiles we see in muggy swamps. Some ran on two legs. Some resembled scaly tigers. One breed of rauisuchian was thirty-three feet long, had curved teeth and an armored body, and ate little dinosaurs for lunch (or breakfast or dinner).

Yep, you read that right: little dinosaurs. The Triassic gave Earth its first dinosaurs, but don't picture a giant *T. rex* or *Argentinosaurus*. Triassic dinos were small and rare. This was not their era of world domination. Mammals arrived on the scene as well and were also little—rat-sized (but not actual rodents). The planet welcomed its first non-insect flying beings. Not birds, not bats, not planes, but flying reptiles called pterosaurs! These were not dinosaurs.

Toward the end of the Triassic, the giant continent of Pangea split up like an angsty boy band. The Atlantic Ocean formed as Europe, Africa, and North America sought some alone time. In the water, coral reefs rebounded after the last extinction, along with different creatures. The first ichthyosaurs, aquatic reptiles that kind of look like dolphins, swam in the seas.

What Likely Happened:

The world's fourth-worst mass extinction is thanks to volcanoes. Again! As Pangea split apart, Earth's crust (the crunchy outer layer of our planet) thinned and fragmented. Volcanic activity went into overdrive along the cracks. Geologists see evidence of this in New Jersey, France, Brazil, and Morocco, which were once all in the same neighborhood. Lava spewed and covered the land, but more tragically, CO_2 again filled the air. Temperatures rose, and oceans acidified. *Climate change!* You get the picture.

Famous Victims:

- Conodonts, which are small marine invertebrates that left behind tooth-looking fossils.
- The enormous croc-like rauisuchians and other large crocodilians. Their reign is over.
- The dolphin-like ichthyosaurs.
- Coral reefs almost go entirely extinct.

HAPPY ENDINGS, KIND OF

Post-Triassic, Earth bounced back yet again. We live on a very resilient planet—at least so far. With the pesky large crocodilians gone, a new king of beasts emerged. Make way! Here. They. Come. Dinosaur-sized dinosaurs!

CHAPTER 3

MASS EXTINCTIONS, CONTINUED
THE FIFTH ONE GOT THE DINOSAURS

MOST POPULAR EXTINCTION

The other mass extinctions are interesting, but they can't compare to the thrilling and exciting event that killed off dinosaurs, IMHO. At least the *non-avian* dinosaurs. Birds are living, breathing, real-life dinosaurs. But let's gently shove them aside for a moment and pay our respects to the dinosaurs that no longer roam.

WELCOME TO THE CRETACEOUS–TERTIARY EXTINCTION!

It's also known as the K-T extinction, even though "Cretaceous" begins with a C. (The *K* stands for the German word *kreide*, which means chalk, and Cretaceous rock is kind of chalky.) Also known as the End-Cretaceous extinction. And more recently, with the term Tertiary being retired and the name Paleogene (66 million to 23 million years ago) being promoted, we get K-Pg extinction for Cretaceous-Paleogene. And some publications even use C-Pg. This book will call it the K-T extinction because we just need to pick a favorite.

Dinosaurs and mammals first appeared on Earth after the Great Dying. These small animals trudged along in the background as the crocodile-like ancestors dominated the planet. But the End-Triassic extinction got rid of the competition, and dinosaurs became the rulers of the land for about the next 135 million years. Mammals continued to scurry underfoot, probably none growing larger than a medium-sized dog. Though some, like the three-foot-long *Repenomamus*, actually ate small (or dead) dinosaurs.

During their reign, dinosaurs grew bigger and bigger. But not all dinosaurs were huge, like *Microraptor*, which was only about the size of a crow. And while dinosaurs existed throughout the 135 million years, individual species came and went. One of my favorite dinosaurs, *Spinosaurus*, went extinct approximately 94 million years ago and wasn't even around at the same time as every preschooler's favorite, *T. rex*. (The "king of the tyrant lizards" took the throne 68 million years ago.) The two dinosaurs would never have met and thus would never have battled. I think *Spinosaurus* would have won in claw-to-claw combat. It was longer and heavier, *and* it could swim.

T. rex also never got a chance to mingle with the stegosauruses, which went belly-up 144 million years ago. Here's some fun math. Let's calculate who is separated by more time: *T. rex* and stegosaurus or *T. rex* and us.

Stegosaurus	144 mya	T. rex	66 mya
T. rex	− 68 mya	Us (Today)	− 0
Difference	76 mya		66 mya

There's less time between humans and the *tyrant lizard* than between the two dinosaurs. Wild!

Even with some species already extinct, plenty of dinosaurs were doing well 66 million years ago. *T. rex* and triceratops hung out in North America. *Argentinosaurus* and *Rinconsaurus* towered across South America. Species diversity may have been declining (meaning there was less variety of dinosaurs), but in general, the dinosaurs weren't in danger of complete extinction. Until...

EARTH'S WORST DAY

We've all had bad days: forgotten our lunch, said goodbye to a beloved pet, had a favorite streaming series canceled. But collectively, this was Earth's worst bad day ever.

Let's time travel to that apocalyptic moment about 66 million years ago, when Earth gets a destructive *visitor* from space. Imagine we're in the western United States, and we're hundreds of miles from Chicxulub, Mexico—the impending crash site. We've arrived a few days before the big impact, giving us some time for sightseeing. It's spring. Or at least it's spring-like because plants are flowering. We notice *T. rex* eating carrion and triceratops grazing. We may also see a

UFO in the sky. This unidentified flying *object* is not an alien spaceship but just an *object*. Scientists cannot definitively tell us whether it was a comet (more icy) or an asteroid (more metallic or rocky). For simplicity, we'll call it an asteroid from here on out because that's what I prefer. This asteroid appears and disappears and terrifies us because we know what's coming. The giant reptiles aren't concerned about the asteroid. At least not until it gets very, very, very close.

On impact day, the 6.2-mile-wide asteroid enters Earth's atmosphere traveling faster than a speeding bullet. Because of the size and velocity, the asteroid compresses the air in front of it. Something big and fast can *crush* air. In the immediate area, the temperature would be hotter than on the sun. At our location in the western United States, we witness a flash of light across the sky. No noise. *Yet!*

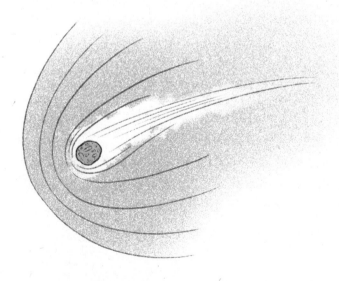

A few seconds later, we experience another, more intense burst of light. This second flash, which is bright enough to burn our retinas, is the actual impact. Still, no sound. This destructive asteroid is so large that the back end still hasn't officially entered Earth's troposphere (the first layer of our atmosphere) when the front end hits land. Its butt is sticking out.

Soon after, the ground around us violently shakes, throwing rocks, trees, dinosaurs, everything (including us time travelers!) into the air. If we used today's Richter scale (which scores earthquakes from zero to ten) to measure this rumble-tumble event, it would be off the charts—let's give it a twelve. The tremors can be felt around the globe. This triggers tsunamis, which crush coastal areas in the Americas with walls of water hundreds of feet high.

As the ground settles and the bounce-house ride ends, the destruction is just ramping up. Across North America, it rains *fire*. That's because, back at the impact site, the asteroid and miles of Earth's crust have been pulverized. The fragments have been flung into the atmosphere. What goes up must come down. The superheated debris falls across the hemisphere. Any animals out in the open get third-degree burns. (Let's imagine we're standing safely under a fireproof umbrella.) Grasses, shrubs, and trees ignite, setting off wildfires. The temperature from this event is hot enough to bake a pizza.

Most large animals in North America—those who cannot find shelter—are dead within the hour.

Let's assume we're unscathed (*thanks, fireproof umbrella*). The next wave of the apocalypse is the wind and the sonic boom. Since light travels faster than sound, we have to wait an hour or more for this. The crash is loud enough to rupture eardrums, even thousands of miles away, and the winds would make a Category 5 hurricane feel like a breeze. This apocalyptic wind drives water over riverbanks and flattens trees.

Not much survives the first few hours, at least in North America. The animals that manage to escape this first wave of destruction must then deal with the smoke from the wildfires and the cloud of debris from the impact blocking out the sun for months, maybe years. Global temperatures dip; it's the beginning of an impact winter. Plants struggle, which means animals that eat plants struggle, and the global food chain falls apart. It's time for us to get out of here. *Everyone, back to our time machine!*

BUT HOW DO WE KNOW ALL THIS?

Humans have been hypothesizing about the cause of the dinosaurs' demise since the first fossils were identified. (The word "dinosaur" came on the scene in 1841, but fossil discoveries date back centuries earlier.) Volcanoes, floods, disease, and dozens of other culprits have all been considered. Even dino poop pollution was suggested. Imagine these huge animals roaming across the countryside, leaving big piles of feces with no poop-scooping service available. *Ick! No thanks!*

It wasn't until 1980 that the asteroid-impact theory gained solid scientific footing. The father-son team of Walter (son) and Luis (dad) Alvarez are credited with the discovery that shook the paleontology world. (We should note that other scientists weren't far behind.) Walter was studying fossils in a rock quarry in Italy when he noticed something peculiar. Scientists already knew that dinosaurs had gone extinct 66 million years ago. They'd examined layers of rocks worldwide and found dinosaur fossils below the rocks that formed 66 million years ago but not above. What Walter discovered was a fine line—or layer—of clay at that transition. Again, below the line, we have dinos, and above, we have none.

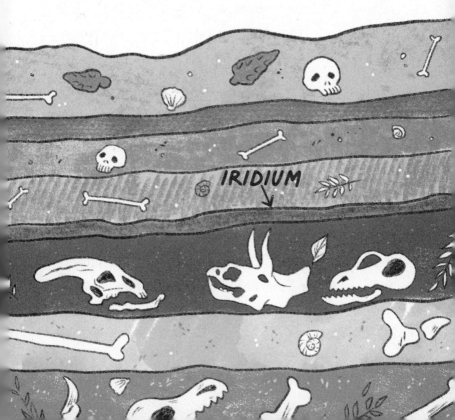

Walter, doing the sensible thing, called his father to talk about this strange find. His dad wasn't just a dad; Luis was a Nobel Prize–winning scientist. (A physicist, to be exact. He won the prize in 1968 for his work with subatomic particles.) The two Alvarezes studied the clay in a lab, and they struck gold. Well, not gold, literally. They struck iridium—a heavy metal that is rare on Earth but plentiful in space. They decided to see if this iridium layer existed beyond the rock quarry in Italy. And it did! They found it across the globe—a thin layer of exotic space metal. That must mean that a huge space rock hit Earth 66 million years ago, vaporized on impact, and left a layer of iridium dust on every continent. This *aha* moment was published as a scientific paper in 1980, and right away, people started asking, "Oh yeah? If there was such a big impact, where's the ginormous crater?"

Good question. The hunt for the impact site began. With Earth being covered by 71 percent water, there was a chance the crater was in the ocean. That would be harder to find, yet not impossible. Finally, in 1991, researchers determined that a giant crater on the Yucatán Peninsula in Mexico was ground zero. Oil companies had known about the divot for decades but assumed an enormous dormant volcano had created it. And since jungles cover most of it and a portion is beneath the Gulf of Mexico, it wasn't like scientists could fly over the spot and say, "Check out that hole."

DID THE CHICXULUB ASTEROID ACT ALONE?

By 2000, scientists had the iridium as evidence *and* the crater as evidence. Most agree that an asteroid hit Earth 66 million years ago, right about when the last *T. rex* went belly-up. Yet some scientists wonder if this collision was enough to wipe out *all* the dinosaurs around the *entire* world. Giant asteroids have hit our planet in the past, and those impacts did not cause mass extinctions. (Like the impact 212 million years ago in Canada that created Lake Manicouagan. An estimated five-mile-wide asteroid made the sixty-mile-wide crater.) So maybe the Chicxulub asteroid got a little help in erasing non-avian dinosaurs from Earth. That help could have come from volcanoes near India. The Deccan Traps had been burping and spewing on and off for 400,000 years. Then here comes a mega asteroid, the likes of which had not been seen in millions of years, and the seismic jolt from the collision could have set the volcanoes into overdrive. Thick lava deposits can be found in the area, but it was the CO_2 that messed everything up. *Climate change! Again!* It was not a good time to be a (non-avian) dinosaur anywhere on the planet.

AFTER THE DINOSAURS

After the Cretaceous-Tertiary extinction, the planet recovered, and new species came to dominate the land, seas, and air. Most of the survivors were small, able to burrow into the ground, fly away, or hole up somewhere safe. Rat-sized

NON-NON-AVIAN DINOSAURS!
(OR AVIAN DINOSAURS!)

Not all dinosaurs are extinct. We still have 10,000 dino species inhabiting Earth. We call them birds. Sometime during the Late Jurassic, birds descended from carnivorous theropods—the same group that gave us velociraptors and tyrannosaurs.

Scientists began searching for the earliest bird descendant right after Charles Darwin published his book about evolution, *On the Origin of Species*, in 1859. Evolution is the theory that living organisms developed from earlier organisms. (Like dogs evolved from wolves.) Essentially, over generations and long periods of time, one species may genetically change enough to become a new species. The new species is usually better adapted or more successful for certain environments or tasks. (Like dogs make better pets than wolves.)

We can't think of evolution as a quick and direct process. If a cat is born with a third eye (through some genetic mutation), that doesn't mean that cat's kittens will have three eyes. And even if having three eyes is better than having two eyes, that doesn't mean the mutation will infiltrate the feline population to create a new species.

Within a few years of Darwin's book, the 150-million-year-old *Archaeopteryx* was discovered and earned the missing-link-between-bird-and-dino title. *Archaeopteryx* had feathered wings, a wishbone, a long bony tail, and a mouth full of teeth, making it appear half dino and half bird. But as more fossils have been unearthed, earlier birds (or proto-birds) have been identified. Scientists now know evolution prefers to take smaller steps over thousands of years. There's no single species linking *T. rex* to the turkey. Bird traits like feathers, wishbones, and wings developed slowly in various species, not all at once in a single awesome beast. Still, without a doubt, birds are dinosaurs! And, fun fact, pterodactyls are neither dinosaur nor bird. (The correct name is pterodactyloids, and they are flying reptiles.)

BA-KAAAW!

DINOSAUR RELATIVE

animals had better odds of survival than even cat-sized critters. But Earth would see giant animals once again. Megafauna (meaning: enormous animals) would spread across the planet, like *Glyptodon*, a mammal similar to an armadillo with a five-foot-long shell and a club-like tail. *Megatherium*, better known as the giant ground sloth, weighed as much as an elephant. *Daeodon*, or "terrible pig," was twelve feet long and 2,000 pounds. And then there were the famous megafauna like woolly mammoths, dire wolves, and saber-toothed tigers. Some of these animals even shared Earth with people, which probably led to the beasts' demise.

We can't avoid it any longer. Let's fast-forward and look at humans. Talk about a big impact!

CHAPTER 4

HOMO SAPIENS

NOT THE ONLY HUMANS

HELLO, HUMAN!

Unless you're reading this aloud to your dog, cat, or pet lemur, let's assume everyone perusing or listening to this book is human. And currently, the only humans living on the planet are *Homo sapiens*.

So, hello, *Homo sapiens*!

(*Homo* is Latin for man. *Sapiens* is Latin for wise.)

But this has not always been the case. To put it simply, a human is an animal under the genus *Homo*. This includes *Homo sapiens, Homo erectus, Homo floresiensis* (sometimes referred to as "hobbits" because of their size), and Neanderthals. The chimpanzee and the bonobo are considered our closest living relatives, and they're in the genus *Pan*. So what makes a human (in the genus *Homo*) different from a creature in the genus *Pan*? It's our big, energy-sucking brains! A human brain requires 25 percent of our energy while the body is at rest (like when you're sitting at your desk doing homework). An ape's brain uses only 8 percent. Humans can also make cool tools. Other animals, like crows and apes, use tools too, but humans invented the waffle maker and the porta potty, so we win.

The question of human origins is a puzzle that anthropologists have been tackling for decades. It's a fun (perhaps unsolvable) mystery. They collect bones, fossils, and tools to identify species and learn about lifestyles. Current evidence points to early humans evolving from *Australopithecus*, or "southern ape," between 2.5 million and 2.8 million years ago. Perhaps the most famous *Australopithecus* is Lucy.

SCIENTIFIC CLASSIFICATION

Species	*Homo sapiens* AKA: person Note: human	*Homo neanderthalensis* AKA: Neanderthal Note: human	*Pan troglodytes* AKA: chimp Note: not human
Genus	*Homo*	*Homo*	*Pan*
Family	Hominidae	Hominidae	Hominidae
Order	Primate	Primate	Primate
Class	Mammalia	Mammalia	Mammalia
Phylum	Chordata	Chordata	Chordata
Kingdom	Animalia	Animalia	Animalia
Domain	Eukaryota	Eukaryota	Eukaryota

MEET LUCY

In 1974, scientists in Ethiopia discovered a 40 percent complete ancient skeleton (trust me, 40 percent is like a jackpot for fossils). They named the specimen Lucy after the Beatles song "Lucy in the Sky with Diamonds," which they listened to that night as they

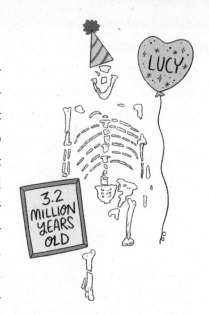

celebrated this incredible find. Lucy is an *Australopithecus afarensis*. She is not in the *Homo* genus and not an early human, but certainly a relative. Lucy is 3.2 million years old. That's a lot of candles for a birthday cake. She stood three feet, seven inches tall, weighed about sixty pounds, and had some apelike characteristics such as long arms, short legs, and a smallish brain. But she also had a humanlike spine, pelvis, and knees, which allowed her to walk around on two legs.

SO WHO ARE THE FIRST HUMANS?

The first *Homo* species may never be known with certainty, but we do know *H. sapiens* did not lead the movement. *Homo erectus* roamed Earth at least 1.5 million years before our species. These humans most likely originated in Africa and spread across Asia and Europe. Compared to us, they had bigger teeth and smaller brains. They were hunters and gatherers who used tools and may have been the first humans to master fire—we know they were burning stuff about a million years ago. The reason for their total disappearance is a mystery. There's no evidence of *H. erectus* and *H. sapiens* interacting, though the time frames overlap slightly. We just weren't in the same place at the same time.

BRING IN THE *SAPIENS*

Homo sapiens (us!) are a newish species. Our arrival is estimated to be around 300,000 years ago. Think about that! Triceratops roamed for 3 million years. Blue whales have swum the ocean for at least 1.5 million years. And even *H. erectus* hunted and foraged for almost 2 million years. As a species, we are newbies. Babies, really.

Like other species of the genus *Homo*, we started in Africa—maybe in Ethiopia, maybe in Morocco, the exact location is up for debate. About 90,000 years ago, we spread out into Eurasia (Europe and Asia's OTP name). We can imagine our great-great-great-great-...grandparents migrated in search of food and new lands. At this point, the most common occupation was hunter-gatherer.

Early *H. sapiens* communities were probably small and very portable. They had to carry everything: shelters, cookware, tools, and little kids. They ate an organic diet of fruits, nuts, and veggies. They also hunted and fished, though this was probably a smaller part of their menu. Hunting takes lots of energy. Have you tried to run down a deer? Early humans went where the food was available. And we can assume there were clashes over the best berries and hunting grounds. As populations expanded, people needed more land to find food.

Neanderthals shared the planet with *H. sapiens* for a time. They lived in colder climates in Europe and central Asia and had bigger brains than *H. sapiens*. You may have seen depictions of Neanderthals as slouching, hairy, bowlegged humans. That's not accurate. This image emerged because one of the first nearly complete Neanderthal skeletons—a dude found in a cave-grave in France—had severe osteoarthritis. That's a condition that causes joint deterioration. Early scholars described Neanderthals as "brutish" and "clumsy" and considered them gorilla-like, not human. More recent finds reveal that Neanderthals had muscular arms and legs, large skulls, and broad chests. These humans were social animals that lived in large family clans. They hunted and gathered. They painted! We see this in caves in Spain from 65,000 years ago. Neanderthals also cared for their sick and used medicinal plants. If a family member was old or unwell, they probably didn't just abandon that person. When one of them died, they seemed to have had ceremonies or burial rituals. Some archeologists believe this could be evidence of religious practices as well.

NO MORE NEANDERTHALS

Neanderthals sound like legit early humans whose offspring should be hanging around with us on the playground today. So what happened? No one knows for sure, but there are theories. Let's start with the most violent one. Early *H. sapiens* may have slaughtered the Neanderthals. We can imagine battles over land and other resources. *H. sapiens* are notorious for violent clashes, so this theory is totally on-brand. From the Crusades to World War II to a fight with your sibling over the last slice of cake, we're capable of destroying others. (Please do not hurt anyone over cake—even really good cake.) Another theory is that *H. sapiens* gobbled up most of the resources without actively fighting the Neanderthals. *H. sapiens* may have hunted all the local animals and eaten all the local vegetation, leaving nothing for anyone else. The final theory is that Neanderthals *joined* the *sapiens* clans. There is evidence to support this. Some modern people can attribute up to 4 percent of their DNA to Neanderthals. Cool, right? You might be part Neanderthal.

Chances are that the demise of the Neanderthals had more than one cause. So we know there was breeding between *H. sapiens* and Neanderthals. (Again, DNA!) But the complete wipeout of the rest of the species was probably due to a combination of reasons—war, lack of resources, maybe throw in an infectious disease too. We may never know the exact cause, but we know they disappeared between 35,000 and

24,000 years ago. Bye-bye to one of our last-living species relatives.

RISE TO THE TOP

If I may be egotistical for a moment, *H. sapiens* run this world. Just ask the Neanderthals and the woolly mammoths. But *H. sapiens* didn't start at the top of the food chain. Early humans had to worry about getting eaten, and they didn't have the weapons and skills to kill big game. We were probably more like vultures than tigers. The meat early humans ate consisted of small animals and carrion (meaning: dead, decaying flesh) that hadn't been polished off by an alpha animal. After a lion finished with the best parts of a gazelle, humans got stuck with the meager remains, like the bones. Our ancestors probably used stone tools to bust open a few gazelle femurs to enjoy the rich marrow. (Plenty of people still eat bone marrow today, but not because it's leftovers from an apex predator.) So how did humans rise to the top?

LET IT BURN

As mentioned, nonhuman animals can create and use tools. Crows fashion twigs into utensils for reaching food. Elephants use branches as fly swatters. And chimpanzees create hammer-like tools and spear-like weapons. But none of these supersmart animals have learned to master fire. (Note: Some animals use fire to their advantage—like birds that drop nuts into flames so the shells will crack—but they don't know how to light a match.) Fire-starting is a human advantage that allows us to cook, stay warm, have light at night, protect ourselves, and dominate nature. Fire could be used to clear land and force prey from the underbrush. Early humans would burn fields, and, if done correctly, all the rabbits and other small critters would go hopping for their lives right into a trap. Then it was rabbit stew for dinner!

While it's convenient to wave a torch to ward off hungry jackals or light a bonfire to keep a clan warm, fire's real advantage is cooking—which saves us a ton of time. Our ape ancestors can spend hours every day chewing their food. Early humans may have done this too. *Chewing, chewing, all the livelong day.* But once humans began cooking their dinners, less time was needed for chewing and digestion. Also, human bellies cannot handle uncooked wheat, rice, or potatoes. Those foods need to be cooked first so we may enjoy their nutrients. High heat also reduces bacteria and other nasty organisms that might live in meats and raw foods.

Fire is not an *H. sapiens* invention. But it's hard to pinpoint the exact moment non-*sapiens* humans started playing with fire. We know, for example, Neanderthals and *H. erectus* mastered the flame, and earlier humans took advantage of naturally occurring fires, maybe as far back as 1.5 million years ago. *H. sapiens* controlled it long before we began world domination. Fire alone did not make us *superior* to other animals. Seven millennia ago, we were still pretty insignificant in the animal kingdom. The real reason for our rise to the top has to do with language.

SAPIENS SPEAK

Nearly all animals communicate. This is not an *H. sapiens* superpower. They can warn of danger, threaten others, and flirt with potential mates. But humans take communication and language to the next level. Sure, our dogs can bark to alert other dogs (and us) that someone is at the front door. But can our dogs communicate that someone *was* at our front door this morning? When we get home, can our dogs say, "Jack stopped by to see if you wanted to play basketball"? Nope. (If *your* dog can do this, I hope you record it and post it online. I want to see!) Our dogs, like all animals, essentially live in the present. Dogs can mark a tree (pee on it) and let other animals know that "Rex was here." But that's not quite the same.

We know non-*sapiens* humans like the Neanderthals were capable of communication. Their brain size and physiology point to this. But unfortunately for Neanderthals, it was a genetic mutation in *H. sapiens* between 70,000 and 30,000 years ago that led to our eventual dominance across the planet. Scientists believe the *H. sapiens'* brains *accidentally* rewired and became capable of sharing information on a whole new level, which gave us two advantages. First, *H. sapiens* languages are incredibly flexible. We can communicate infinite ideas: directions to the grocery store, details about World War II battles, solutions to equations, and how to beat the final boss in a video game. The second advantage: We gained the ability to tell stories. *H. sapiens* could connect sounds to create an unlimited number of sentences and connect those sentences to create tales.

Stories aren't always fiction, and they aren't just for entertainment. With this *new* brain, *H. sapiens* were able to gossip about friends and family. "Don't trust Zeke. He's a cheater."

This allowed *H. sapiens* to create larger communities and work together more efficiently than earlier humans. Suddenly, they didn't need to know everyone in their community personally. They just needed to know their reputation. Eventually, using our advanced language and rewired brains, *H. sapiens* added religion, economics, writing, and government.

We can't say why our brains changed. We just get to enjoy the benefits.

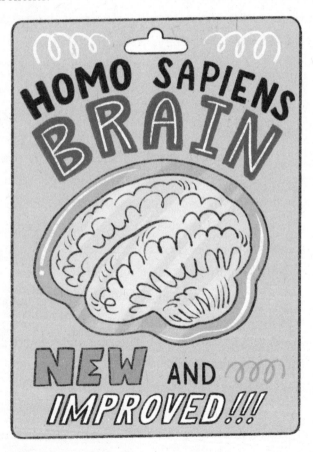

TIME TO SETTLE DOWN

The first non-nomadic societies began near good fishing holes. A steady supply of seafood meant humans could settle down and start villages. But people became real-estate obsessed only 12,000 years ago with the development of farming. At first glance, this might sound like a great idea. Let's take some seeds, and instead of eating them all, let's plant them in the ground and make more food. *Brilliant! What an investment!* Humans were able to feed more people while staying in one place. But it turns out that farming is hard work, especially before the invention of tractors, pesticides, and sprinklers. In the beginning, humans had few domesticated animals to help out. An ancient farmer's workday was probably longer than that of a nomad's. Also, with the rise of farming, human diets became less varied. If we grow corn, we eat mostly corn. If we grow rice, we eat mostly rice. If we grow pizza, we eat mostly pizza. (We cannot live on pizza alone. For a balanced diet, we need salad too.) Compare this to the nomad life, in which we eat whatever we come across. Another downside: Farming led to inequality. Landowners rose to the top of the society's ladder, while others toiled in the field for little reward.

Still, farming allowed us to feed more mouths, and with advanced techniques, fewer people were required for the job. This led humans to pursue other careers, like hatmaker, butcher, doctor, queen, scientist, and YouTube star.

For a species that's been roaming Earth for only 300,000-ish years, we've made a remarkable impact. We live on all the continents and have visited the moon. Our population is booming; we should be 11 billion strong by 2100. We have science and art, money and religion, Netflix and books. Team *Homo sapiens* seems unstoppable....

But there *was* this one time when we were kind of close to extinction. Our species—like so many others—could have ended up just fossils.

CHAPTER 5

DNA BOTTLENECK

THAT TIME HUMANS ALMOST WENT EXTINCT

We know all non-*sapiens* humans are extinct. Neanderthals and *Homo erectus* are no longer walking this Earth. Only *Homo sapiens* has prevailed—so far. But something happened about 70,000 years ago that could have wiped us off this planet.

DOWN TO A FEW THOUSAND

Scientists have studied our DNA and have determined that *H. sapiens* went through a bottleneck somewhere prior to 60,000 years ago. As our ancestors moved out of Africa, their population significantly declined. The exact number is unknown, but researchers estimate that the human herd size was between 3,000 and 10,000 individuals. That would put us on an endangered species list. Modern humans may have descended from a group so small it wouldn't even fill every seat in a football stadium.

This means that we are all quite genetically similar. If we randomly chose two humans today and compared their DNA, they would be 99.9 percent identical. Our two test subjects may be different sizes, different races, different genders, different religions, and have different tastes in music. Still, they will always be only .1 percent different from each other genetically. (That means 999 out of 1,000 genes will be the same.)

H. sapiens aren't the only animals that experienced a genetic bottleneck during this time frame. Chimpanzees, tigers, and orangutans also have DNA that indicates they are the offspring of a few hardy critters. So what happened that trimmed the branches of our genetic tree? Honestly, scientists don't know. One (highly controversial!) hypothesis was a massive volcanic explosion. BOOOOM!

TOBA

Approximately 74,000 years ago, a mountain in Indonesia on the island of Sumatra blew its lid. This former mountain—which is now a beautiful lake—was named Toba, and it was the most massive volcanic eruption in the last 2 million years. And the largest witnessed by humans.

It's likely Toba rumbled and grumbled for months, maybe even years, before the main event. When it finally erupted, ash and debris—including boulders—shot into the atmosphere, with the eruption cloud reaching nineteen miles high. (For reference, airplanes fly five to seven miles above the ground.)

The flowing lava may have raced down the mountain at sixty miles per hour. Cars go that fast. Humans do not. The sound of the eruption may have been heard around the world.

The ash ejected into the sky spread across the northern and southern hemispheres. A layer of soot six inches deep fell over the Indian subcontinent, but the accumulation reached twenty feet in some places. That much ash would certainly close schools for the day, if only there were schools around.

Another ejected material from Toba was sulfuric acid. *Yuck*. This chemical choked the skies, and when mixed with water, it created acid rain—an ingredient not desired in any recipe. Depending on acidity levels, acid rain can strip trees of foliage, destroy fish and reptile eggs, and make soil lousy for plant growth.

The initial effects of Toba would have been horrible in the immediate area. Good thing *H. sapiens* were still mainly in Africa, with maybe a smattering in southern Asia. Few humans (probably none) were running down the mountain, trying to outrace the lava flow. However, as we've seen so often in past extinctions, volcanic eruptions can have lingering and far-reaching catastrophic effects. Did Toba make a lasting impact?

VOLCANIC WINTER?

Ice is one of Earth's best time capsules. Each year, new layers form on glaciers, capturing geological and environmental data. Scientists can drill into the ice and take core samples by extracting long cylindrical pieces. At the top of the cylinder is today and at the bottom is ancient history. (One sample "went back" 2.7 million years.) Using an ice core from Greenland, scientists looked at tiny air bubbles from the Toba time frame and took measurements. They found that Earth was getting colder.

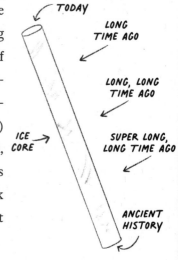

TODAY

LONG TIME AGO

LONG, LONG TIME AGO

ICE CORE

SUPER LONG, LONG TIME AGO

ANCIENT HISTORY

The Toba hypothesis argues that the debris from the eruption blocked sunlight from reaching Earth's surface—maybe for years. Temperatures could have dropped dramatically, some estimates say by as much as 18°F (10°C). That would be like Florida suddenly feeling like Maine. The lack of sunny rays wouldn't have only made life chilly, but it would also interfere with plant growth because photosynthesis requires sunlight. There's a domino effect with this too. Fewer plants growing. Fewer animals eating plants. Less meat for carnivores (and omnivores). Life on Earth may have become quite tricky, causing *H. sapiens* numbers to dwindle. *(Hello, bottleneck!)* Only the hardiest—and luckiest—would have survived.

OR MAYBE TOBA IS NOT TO BLAME

While Toba is a fun explanation for our lack of genetic diversity, and it was once a popular theory, there is plenty of science that says, "Hold on a second!" Toba certainly did erupt between 70,000 and 75,000 years ago, and it was massive, but the impact on humans may not have been wildly significant.

Let's look at the ice again. When scientists examined those cylindrical samples, they noticed that those layers from 74,000 years ago did not contain ash. If volcanic debris blocked out sunlight around the world and caused winter to last for years, then we should see this sediment in the ice. But it's not there! The air bubbles trapped in the ice show the temperature drop, but new studies suggest the cooling was only in the northern hemisphere and only for a short time.

HUMAN EVIDENCE

Ice is not the only evidence that points to Toba being a not-huge deal. Researchers working at Pinnacle Point in South Africa discovered human settlements that thrived post-cataclysm. Unlike the ice cores in Greenland, this location has an ash layer, indicating the Toba impact. The archeologists found over 400,000 human artifacts in the ash layer *and* in the layers above and below the ash—meaning the Pinnacle Point humans kept calm and carried on before, during, and after Toba.

Closer to the eruption, at the Dhaba dig site in Madhya Pradesh, India, archeologists found primitive stone tools that date back to before Toba's eruption *and* after, giving us additional evidence that humans survived this supervolcano. It should be pointed out that the humans at this location were probably not *H. sapiens,* who were still hanging out only in Africa. Only tools have been found (not bones or remains), so this tribe could be another known species of *Homo* or even an unknown species.

If the humans living within 2,000 miles of Sumatra survived the Toba eruption, then humans across Africa, Europe, and Asia were probably not terribly inconvenienced by the largest volcano ever in human history. Or maybe the humans of the Dhaba site were more adaptable than other humans, like a tribe of Phineases and Ferbs.

All we know for sure is that Toba erupted violently about 74,000 years ago, and sometime before 60,000 years ago, *Homo sapiens* numbers were significantly reduced, causing a genetic bottleneck. More scientific discoveries are necessary to prove (or disprove) whether the two are related. Still, this is the closest *H. sapiens* have come to extinction in 300,000 years. Since then, we've gone from a few thousand in number to nearly 8 billion. But does that mean our time of doom won't come? Are we safe from extinction?

Eh, probably not.

PART II

IN THE FUTURE

A FEW OF MY FAVORITE THREATS

Humans are not invincible—just ask the Neanderthals. Our species could (will?) eventually follow in the footprints of dinosaurs, passenger pigeons, and northern white rhinos. *Extinction!* It's estimated 99 percent of all animal species that have ever lived on Earth are now gone. Is it just a matter of time before we join the majority?

In this section, we'll look at the threats that could—but hopefully won't—make fossils of the *Homo sapiens* species. Some risks come from outer space, some lurk close by, and some we've managed to create on our very own. Let's explore what threatens our existence, and what (if any!) steps we can take to prevent looming disasters.

CHAPTER 6

ASTEROIDS

INCOMINGGGGG!

WE'RE UNDER ATTACK!

Earth is pelted by approximately 100 tons of space rock every day. But we have the ultimate defense mechanism. Our atmosphere! This layer of gases is a mighty force field protecting us from ongoing space attacks. It's worth noting that these daily meteoroids are mostly small, like pebbles, or even smaller, like grains of sand. Our atmosphere devours these little pests. Occasionally, slightly larger space rocks attempt to crash-land on Earth, and still, our atmosphere is like, "Don't sweat it. I got this." When these pieces burn up in our sky, they can create bright streaks of light, which should be referred to as meteors, not as "shooting stars." But feel free to make a wish on them, if you'd like.

WELL-BEHAVED ASTEROIDS VS. ROGUE ASTEROIDS

But enough of the small and (literally) everyday stuff. Let's look at the world-ending giants soaring through our planetary neighborhood. Most asteroids are as old as our solar system, having formed about 4.6 billion years ago. Asteroids, also called planetoids, mainly hang out in the asteroid belt between Mars and Jupiter. They happily sail around and don't usually bother planets or planetary inhabitants. But occasionally, Jupiter's or Mars's gravity knocks one of these millions of asteroids out of its loop. *Uh-oh!* An asteroid that's no longer cruising in its designated lane has three options.

1. It can (eventually) crash into the sun.
2. It can leave our solar system and live out a lonely existence in the Milky Way.
3. It can collide with a planet, or a moon, or a dwarf planet, or a space station.

So what happens if one of these rogue asteroids sets its sights on planet Earth? If it's a big one, the good news is that we'll see it. In 1998, Congress told NASA to find 90 percent of the near-Earth objects (NEOs) over one kilometer (.62 miles) wide within a decade. NASA, the overachievers that they are, exceeded that goal and found 95 percent. Using computer modeling, they can predict if any of these asteroids pose a threat to our planet. And NASA is not just making predictions for the next seven days, like your local weather forecast. They're calculating the path of these massive rocks for the next 100 years. In other good news, NASA is confident that none of these giant asteroids will pay us a visit in the next century.

THINGS FROM SPACE (SOME THAT COULD WIPE OUT HUMANITY)

Asteroid—a space object that's mostly rocky and metallic, originating in the asteroid belt and born at the same time as our solar system

Comet—an icy space rock that probably formed in the farthest reaches of our solar system; has a dust tail and is surrounded by a cloud of gas and dust called a coma

Meteor—the streak or flash of light caused by a space rock burning up in our atmosphere, sometimes called a "shooting star," which is technically incorrect

Meteorite—a piece of space rock that lands on Earth

Meteoroid—a space object that's not as big as an asteroid or comet, but was likely once a part of an asteroid or comet

AN (IMAGINARY) ASTEROID NAMED BETTY

Let's imagine that a never-before-noticed asteroid (one of the 5 percent NASA missed) comes on the scene and wants to make Earth its permanent home. Since asteroids don't glow from within—they reflect the sun's light, just like planets and moons—it's possible telescopes could overlook a large dark asteroid, especially if it's coming at us from the direction of the sun. Ever try to catch a baseball while looking up at the sun? It's kind of like that. But we wouldn't miss a giant asteroid completely. Scientists estimate that in the worst-case scenario, we'd still have three days' warning.

Let's call our fictional near-Earth asteroid (NEA) Betty, after my grandmother, and let's say Betty is one mile across.

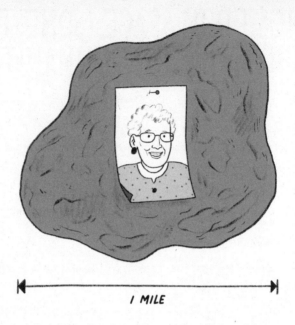

1 MILE

Once astronomers discover Betty, they'll be able to specify an impact zone but not a bullseye. Since our world is 71 percent ocean, a splash landing is most likely. (As you may recall from Chapter 3, the Chicxulub asteroid was a partial water impact...but that still didn't help *T. rex*.) A watery crash within sixty miles of a shoreline would result in tsunamis. A giant wall of water as tall as the Empire State Building could wipe out coastal cities. Islands could go the way of the mythical Atlantis and be completely washed away.

If Betty avoided the oceans and instead made landfall, the impact would be even more devastating. One study suggests it would be ten times more destructive. So let's imagine that! Betty will enter our atmosphere traveling well above the posted speed limit, probably around 50,000 miles per hour.

Anything in the impact radius will be obliterated, leaving behind only a barren crater. Buildings, trees, animals, humans, cell phone towers, and even underground bunkers wouldn't stand a chance against a direct hit. You can imagine the destruction in Denver, Dallas, Detroit, Des Moines, or your hometown (even if it doesn't begin with *D*).

Only about 3 percent of Earth's land is considered urban or densely populated. That means a land-bound Betty has only a one in thirty-three chance of striking a city. But just because a metropolis escapes a direct hit doesn't mean its inhabitants are out of the woods. Betty crashing anywhere on land will result in high-speed wind, shock waves, earthquakes, fires, and years-long apocalyptic conditions. Similar to what the dinosaurs went through, except we have more stuff to break.

The wind and shock waves alone will be responsible for 60 percent loss of life, both human and animal. The wind speeds could reach 1,000 miles per hour. For reference, a gust of forty to forty-five miles per hour can lift a 100-pound person. The post-Betty shock waves will have the potential to rupture your organs. *Ick!*

Earthquakes won't pack the same deadly punch as wind and shock waves, but they'll be massive and will be experienced in parts of the world that rarely feel even tiny tremors. The ground will move up and down several feet, which could topple buildings, trigger rockslides and avalanches, reroute rivers, and certainly mess with your afternoon carpool.

(Lucky dinosaurs! They didn't have to worry about their roads and buildings being destroyed.)

On impact, Betty would have been blown to bits (RIP asteroid Betty), sending chunks of Earth's crust and pieces of asteroid into the atmosphere at high speeds. This debris will rain back down as burning glass and make the surrounding environment toasty. It will be hot enough to bake cookies outside, which also means our bodies will roast like Thanksgiving turkeys. Water will quickly evaporate at these temperatures, and spontaneous fires will break out across the dry land. Everything within hundreds of miles will become kindling.

Just like with the dino-destroying asteroid, the aftermath of big Betty's boom will be endless gray skies and acid rain. This is terrible weather for going to the beach, and really terrible weather for long-term survival. The sun will be blocked out for years, and the world will experience a decades-long impact winter. That means no spring, summer, and fall for planting, growing, and harvesting. (Just forget about your summer vacation.) Even natural foliage—ya know, the stuff bunnies and deer eat—will stop growing. And if you prefer burgers to salads, you will still go hungry because the cow between your hamburger buns will have nothing to eat either.

SMALLER THAN BETTY BUT STILL SCARY

A Betty-sized asteroid strike (which is seriously unlikely) would probably not wipe *Homo sapiens* off the planet. I'd like to think some of us would survive on bottled water and beef jerky until the impact winter ended. So let's not worry about that. Let's concern ourselves with smaller-than-Betty, more common, locally devastating asteroid strikes.

Dear readers, let me tell you a real-life story.

The date was February 15, 2013. The setting was Chelyabinsk, Russia. Children were at school. Adults were at work or doing other adult things like running errands, watching TV, and texting. Suddenly, a giant flash, brighter than the sun, burst across the clear blue sky. The meteoroid exploded (thanks, atmosphere!) and left a cloud of debris. Now remember, it was February, and it was Russia, so it was freezing cold. Most people were inside, but the bright flash got their attention. They ran to the windows for a better look. Since light travels faster than other waves, like sound, thousands of people were standing near glass as the resulting shock wave came barreling along. The wave shattered glass and damaged hundreds of buildings. Over a thousand people went to the hospital for treatment, mostly for cuts caused by broken glass. No one was injured directly by the space rock.

Scientists estimate the Chelyabinsk meteoroid was initially sixty-five feet across—or almost two school buses long. Most of it broke up fourteen miles above the city—or about twice as high as a plane flies. The largest remaining chunk, 1,000 pounds of ancient solar-system debris, landed in a frozen lake. Impact in a frozen lake is a good outcome. Impact in a bustling city would be disastrous.

Wait! I haven't even told you my favorite part of the story yet.

On this day, February 15, 2013, an asteroid called 2012 DA14 was also passing close to Earth. Researchers had calculated that DA14 would come within 17,000 miles of our planet. (For perspective, the moon is about 240,000 miles from us.) All the astronomers in all the land had pointed their telescopes toward the sky to see DA14, and no one spotted the Chelyabinsk meteoroid until it was visible with the naked eye. That's zero minutes of warning. There are two reasons for this miss. First, the Chelyabinsk rock was too small for 2013 technology to spot. Second, the meteoroid came from the direction of the sun, and suddenly, we had that scenario of catching the pop fly on a sunny day. Scientists missed the ball.

So while NASA and its spacey partners are confident they know about the biggest, *baddest* space rocks, and our atmosphere can gobble up the smallest ones, on occasion, we're going to get hit.

THE BEST DEFENSE

In good news, deaths by space rock are rare—almost unheard-of in modern times. (You're very unlikely to get struck by one while riding your bike.) But a recent investigation found compelling evidence of a meteorite killing one man and paralyzing another on August 22, 1888, in Iraq. Researchers discovered three documents about the event but not the *weapon* itself. Nonhumans are more common victims of space attacks. On May 1, 1860, a horse was fatally struck, and in 1984, a mailbox in Claxton, Georgia, took a beating. Except for the man in Iraq, humans have escaped deadly consequences thus far.

If NASA *does* identify a giant asteroid on a collision course with Earth, what is the best defense? Perhaps a good offense? Nope! Blowing up an asteroid—with nukes or other bombs— would not be ideal. That would make many smaller meteoroids, a majority of which could still seek Earth as their forever home. And gravity could pull some of the fragments back together, re-creating the asteroid. (Also, in 1967, 105 nations signed the Outer Space Treaty, which forbids the use of nuclear weapons in space—though this bit of paperwork would probably not be the most significant obstacle if humanity hung in the balance.)

Instead of blowing up an asteroid, the preferred solution is nudging the rock off its collision course. We could alter the direction of the asteroid, or we could change its speed. A bomb activated near—not on—the asteroid might provide enough of a jolt to do the trick. Similarly, we could push the asteroid off its trajectory for Earth using a small spacecraft powered by solar sails (picture huge boat sails made of mirrorlike material that rely on sunlight instead of wind). Another fun idea involves paint. Imagine pelting one side of the asteroid with white paintballs. The dark half of the asteroid would become warmer from absorbing light, and the lighter half would become cooler, causing a change in the asteroid's speed.

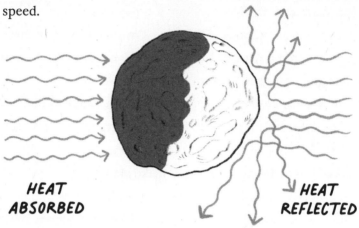

HEAT ABSORBED

HEAT REFLECTED

TESTING, TESTING, ONE, TWO, THREE

It seems that we have different options for preventing a civilization-destroying asteroid strike, but so far, they're all theoretical; none have been tested. That's about to change! In fall 2022, NASA's first planetary defense mission will get a shot at making history.

The Double Asteroid Redirection Test (DART) spacecraft will target a duel asteroid system—specifically Dimorphos, the smaller of the two. Dimorphos is only about .1 miles (160 meters) across and orbits the five-times-bigger asteroid Didymos. The DART impactor will crash into Dimorphos head-on with the assistance of onboard cameras. This self-driven vehicle is about the size of a washing machine, not including the solar arrays. If successful, Dimorphos's orbit around Didymos will be slowed by several minutes. Astronomers on Earth (6.8 million miles away) will be anxiously looking through telescopes for this change in speed.

Reminder, this is a test and only a test. Dimorphos and Didymos are not a threat to Earth. There's no chance of impact (with or without the DART mission). NASA is just trying out technology the dinosaurs wished they had.

NIGHTMARE ON YOUR STREET

Should you lose sleep worrying about asteroids? No. But you could lose sleep observing asteroids. The night sky is the best time to see meteors. Of the threats mentioned in this book, extinction-causing asteroids are one of the easiest to predict. And if we do locate a potentially hazardous object (PHO), we'd likely have years to prepare a defense. The smaller, sneaky meteoroids still pose a threat, just not a global one. And as technology improves, these little rocks might also become more predictable, like snowstorms and hurricanes.

ACRONYMS

Near-Earth object (NEO)—an asteroid or comet whose track will come within 30 million miles of Earth's orbit

Near-Earth asteroid (NEA)—an NEO that is specifically an asteroid (99 percent of NEOs are NEAs)

Potentially hazardous object (PHO)—an asteroid or comet whose track will come within 5 million miles of Earth's orbit and is also greater than 500 feet wide

CHAPTER 7

SUPERVOLCANOES

THE BLAST FROM BELOW

Is there any doubt that volcanic eruptions are catastrophic, deadly events? As we've seen, a majority of Earth's mass extinctions can say "thank you" to volcanic activity, at least in part. The power to change and destroy the environment with extraordinary efficiency is what makes volcanoes so terrifying.

A YEAR WITHOUT SUMMER

We've already been introduced to Toba—the largest eruption in human history. That event was well before written records, and the details are both inferred from scientific evidence *and* disputed using scientific evidence. Let's visit a more recent eruption, complete with witness accounts.

In April 1815, Mount Tambora in Indonesia erupted, triggering events that lasted more than a year. The initial explosion, hot pyroclastic flows (more on this soon), and accompanying tsunamis instantly killed 10,000 people. But that was just the beginning. More than thirty-six cubic miles of debris was ejected into the atmosphere, blocking sunlight and affecting the weather. On the surrounding islands, approximately 80,000 more people died of starvation and disease.

The ash and debris from Tambora spread, creating a kind of cloud over the northern hemisphere. This reduced the amount of sunlight reaching Earth's surface, and the planet's average temperature dropped 5.4°F (3°C). A year later, in the summer of 1816, the climate change effects were felt around the world.

In New England, it snowed in June. Frost and ice killed crops in Maine and Pennsylvania as late as July. There are stories of people eating raccoons and pigeons because food was scarce. In Europe, food riots broke out as well as an epidemic of typhus—a potentially deadly bacterial disease spread by body lice. People, especially those who didn't have a lot of money, were starving across North America and Europe. (And even the well-off were *suffering*. Mary Shelley wrote the horror story *Frankenstein* that year, during her gloomy summer vacation.) At the time, no one associated "the year without summer" with the massive volcano from the previous April. But we now know that this single natural event killed millions worldwide. If it happened today, would we be better prepared?

SUPERVOLCANOES AND VEI

Volcanoes are ranked in awesomeness on the Volcanic Explosivity Index (VEI) with values from zero to eight. Technically, the scale can exceed eight. It just never has. A nine would be ten times worse than an eight. The primary factor that determines a volcano's VEI is the ejecta volume (the amount of stuff coming out of the volcano). Scientists also take into account the height of the eruption column and how long it lasts.

Supervolcanoes are an eight (or higher) on the VEI scale. These are the biggest, the baddest, and the most capable of ending civilization. However, "supervolcano" is not a term most geologists embrace. It's more of a Hollywood word, which became especially popular after a 2005 made-for-TV movie about Yellowstone titled *Supervolcano*. Scientists prefer "super eruption" when referring to a VEI-8 volcano. In this book, we will continue to use "supervolcano," knowing it's not a scientific word but more like extinction slang.

YELLOWSTONE

In 1872, Yellowstone was established as America's first national park. Its fascinating landscape includes geysers—some *faithful* and some on a more erratic schedule—mud pots, hot springs, and the enormous Yellowstone Caldera (a crater approximately thirty by forty-five miles that includes Yellowstone Lake). The park is also famous for its animals, like wolves, bison, brown bears, and a human volcanologist. Okay, maybe the volcanologist isn't as famous as the other critters. The park requires this scientist because it has a history of major eruptions. In the past 2.1 million years, the area has had three big ones, and it's possible the park will see another super eruption. Someday.

But let's imagine that someday is now. Yellowstone sits on two large chambers of magma (AKA: hot molten rock). That's why it has the geysers and the hot springs. Geothermal activity

SOME OF THE WORST

Name and Location	Date	VEI	Fun Frightening Fact
Yellowstone, USA	640,000 years ago	8	One of three large Yellowstone eruptions.
Toba, Indonesia	74,000 years ago	8	Humans were around for this one and, evidently, survived.
Mount Vesuvius, Italy	79 CE	5	Destroyed Pompeii and also preserved this ancient city under the dust and debris.
Ilopango, El Salvador	450 CE	6	Destroyed many Mayan cities and killed over 100,000.
Laki, Iceland	1783 CE	6	One in four people in Iceland died. Caused a famine as far away as Egypt.
Mount Tambora, Indonesia	1815 CE	7	Worst in recorded history.
Krakatoa, Indonesia	1883 CE	6	Krakatoa was uninhabited, but the eruption triggered tsunamis that killed 36,000 and reached as far as South America.
Mount Pelée, Caribbean	1902 CE	4	Of the 28,000 people living on Saint-Pierre, only two survived.
Mount Saint Helens, Washington State	1980 CE	5	We can see footage from this event on the internet. Fifty-seven people died.

at its finest. Every day, more and more magma from deep inside Earth fills these chambers miles below the ground. As long as there's room, and the pressures from above ground and below ground stay the same, all is hunky-dory. But when this buildup becomes too much and the giant magma-filled zit is ready to burst, our first indication of impending doom will be some major earthquakes. The Yellowstone volcanologist is on the lookout for these big-time vibrations. In 2017, several moderate earthquakes shook the area, and some conspiracy enthusiasts thought the supervolcano was on its way. The scientists said nope, nothing to worry about. And they were right.

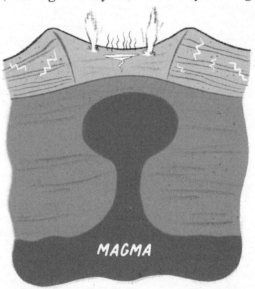

MAGMA

Back to our hypothetical scenario. Let's imagine our quakes are big enough to worry the volcanologist, and they press the evacuate button. (There's no actual button, though.) All the tourists—including us—are ordered to go home because an eruption is coming.

If our twenty-first-century Yellowstone eruption is an eight on the VEI scale, we'd better drive hours outside the park. Lava flow will decimate the immediate area, though it won't travel much beyond the park's borders—based on the past three eruptions. However, we have other problems, thanks to the rock, ash, and gases ejected miles into the air.

Huge volcanoes—like our potential Yellowstone eruption—can be accompanied by a *nuée ardente*, which means "glowing avalanche." Scientists call it pyroclastic flow. It's a lethal mixture of hot gas, ash, rocks, and debris that speeds down the volcanic slope. This burning avalanche can race across the landscape at fifty miles per hour and reach 1,300°F (704°C). Everything in its path, including Yellowstone's wolves, bison, and brown bears, will be incinerated.

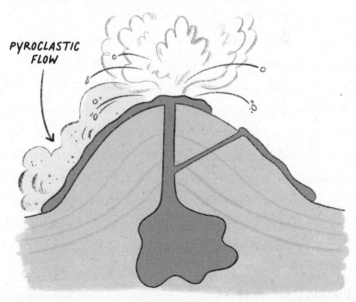

PYROCLASTIC
FLOW

If we escape the lava and the pyroclastic flow, next we'll deal with the volcanic ash in the air. When we take a deep breath, our lungs will fill with volcanic dust, including tiny glass-like shards that will shred the tissues in our respiratory system. In other words, the air will be poisonous. Pain and death will follow.

In the states surrounding Yellowstone, ashfall will be a major issue. The debris that flew into the air will float back down like snow—if snow were toxic and deadly. And volcanic ash is not light and powdery like campfire ash. It's heavy. Just four inches will cause roofs to collapse, and half that amount can cause crops to die. Even less than a quarter inch of ash could contaminate pastures. Cows that eat from those fields would have severe gut pain and likely die. An accumulation on a mountain or glacier can also cause mudflows or avalanches. We've already had to outrun lava and pyroclastic flow, and now this!

After days of driving, we've escaped all these immediate dangers, and we've made it to the Carolinas. But life will still not return to normal. The debris high in the atmosphere will mess up weather patterns. Temperatures will plummet, and some locations will experience droughts. Where it does rain, the water will be contaminated with volcanic gases like sulfur dioxide, creating acid rain. And even the East Coast won't be spared ashfall. New York City, Washington, DC, and Atlanta could all see a trace (about one-tenth of an inch), and that can still cause havoc. In normal times, the water coming from our kitchen tap (unless your home has a well) is cleaned up in a treatment plant. However, the ash in the wastewater will destroy the equipment used in these facilities, and then we will all get very, very thirsty.

The impact from a Yellowstone eruption will reach across North America. In the past, the United States has been able to handle localized natural disasters. If a hurricane hits the East Coast, the rest of the country can send help—food, water, supplies, and volunteers. The same thing happens when an earthquake hits the West Coast. But imagine the entire country hurting. We already know the water will be dirty. Electricity will also likely be knocked out in large portions of the continent. Store shelves will be empty because of damage to farms in the Midwest and issues with transportation, like fuel shortages at gas stations and roadways blocked with volcanic ash.

Hawaii will probably be okay. But they do import a lot of essential supplies from the mainland.

North America's climate will be affected long term by a Yellowstone eruption too. Temperatures will drop because debris in the atmosphere will limit sunlight. (We've seen this scenario many times before.) More crops will fail. Animals and people will go hungry. This cold spell could last for years, maybe up to a decade, and other continents might not be spared.

A super eruption in Yellowstone could devastate the United States. That might be hard to fathom, but let's look at history, and this time I'm not talking about mass extinctions. Some scientists believe that the Okmok volcano eruption in Alaska in 43 BCE helped end the Roman Republic. In March of the previous year, Julius Caesar was assassinated—totally unrelated to the volcano. Then, after the eruption, the weather got wacky, the sun didn't shine, and the citizens starved. Of course, the good people of the republic had no idea that a volcano had exploded on the other side of the world. Some probably thought killing Caesar—who was popular with the people but not the Senate—brought about these tragedies. Admittedly, the fall of the Roman Republic and the rise of the Holy Roman Empire is more complicated than one paragraph can capture. But a volcano did likely make life challenging.

PREPAREDNESS

Most people are probably not prepared for a supervolcano. It's hard to get excited about something that hasn't happened in our lifetime—and by lifetime, I'm referring to the lifetime of modern humans. However, nations and governments are not well prepared either. What the United States spends on volcanic safeguards is a fraction of what we spend on asteroid-impact readiness. NASA's planetary defense budget is about $150 million. The volcano hazard program gets $22 million. And remember, we have a potential supervolcano in our backyard.

Supervolcanoes (and the climate change that always follows) have the potential to cause the next mass extinction.

Even with improving technologies like lasers and thermal imaging, we're not great at predicting eruptions. Earthquakes will certainly give humans some warning, but that's only a few days' notice (whereas with most asteroids, we could have years of warning). And unlike with potential space-rock threats, we don't have any legitimate way to stop a super eruption. Our only defense is to run.

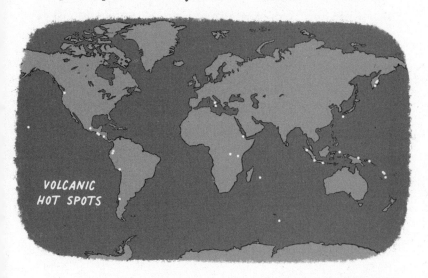

VOLCANIC HOT SPOTS

Still, scientists have considered fun (yet impractical) ideas like cooling magma hot spots. The plan would involve drilling down to the magma chamber and pumping in cold water. There are a couple of problems with this. We don't have equipment that can dig that deep, and it would take thousands of years to pump in enough cold water to cool the magma. (Imagine filling the Grand Canyon with a garden hose. Kinda like that.)

While we cannot stop a VEI 8 eruption, countries could spend more money on research and general preparedness. Emergency provisions of water, food, and medicine are never a bad idea for any of the scenarios we're exploring—both on a community level and a household level.

The chance of a super eruption on any single day is minuscule, and the odds of Yellowstone blowing up this year are one in 730,000. In the past 10,000 years, we've had no VEI 8s and only four VEI 7s. But the chance of a VEI 8 (or greater!) eruption in the next 100,000 years is nearly guaranteed—based on history and what we know about plate tectonics and geology. Just because modern, Wi-Fi–loving *Homo sapiens* have never experienced the fury of a supervolcano does not mean we never will.

CHAPTER 8

DISEASE

TEENY TINY THREATS LIKE BACTERIA AND VIRUSES

We've lived during a pandemic! When I first dreamed of writing this book, I never thought I'd use such a sentence. But here we are, the survivors of the COVID-19 pandemic that began in early 2020. This worldwide event changed life for humans across the globe in small ways and big ways—in the short term and the long term—and killed millions. The reality of a virus wreaking havoc on our lives may be too raw for some readers. If you want to skip this chapter, you're not going to hurt my feelings. And truth be told, while this is Chapter 8, I actually wrote it last.

Let's start with some positive news. A single disease isn't going to wipe out every last *Homo sapiens*. Viruses or bacteria are unlikely to cause our mass extinction. But every person lost is still a tragedy. Let's travel through time and visit some of the valiant attempts by diseases to rid the world of humans.

THE PLAGUE (BACTERIA)

This very efficient killer has spread across continents multiple times over centuries. Scientists have found DNA evidence of the disease in Neolithic farmers from 4,900 years ago, and it probably existed before that time, based on ancient stories. Perhaps the most famous outbreak was the bubonic plague in fourteenth-century Europe, which earned the nickname the Black Death (1347–1351). It's estimated that this outbreak wiped out 60 percent of the European population—or about 50 million people.

We now know that the plague is a bacterium spread by fleas that mainly live on black rats. These biting pests—the fleas, not the rats—infect their hosts with *Yersinia pestis*. Rodents are not immune to this bacterium. They get infected and die. Once the entire rodent colony is wiped out, the hungry fleas need to eat something—or someone—else. About three days after all the rats are dead, the fleas begin to feast on another nearby mammal. Humans.

The black rat, unfortunately, isn't very shy and has always lived among people. This rodent is also a world traveler. The rats (along with the fleas and bacteria) voyaged along trade routes and hit port towns hard. But the disease was not confined to just the cities. It eventually spread to rural areas too. The plague infected and killed nobility, powerful religious leaders, and people of every status. Some, usually the wealthy and educated, tried to escape to country homes in less populated areas. Isaac Newton left Trinity College to spend a few years at his family estate. Although Isaac Newton did survive while a quarter of London's population died, fleeing (or flea-ing—get it?) didn't always work because rats travel everywhere too. Even though the plague did not discriminate, communities without a lot of money or resources were hardest hit because of poor living conditions, overcrowding, and no means of escape.

Once a bacterium-carrying flea bit a human, it took two to six days for the person to show symptoms of bubonic plague. The lymph nodes in the groin, thighs, neck, or armpits would painfully swell with liquid, creating lumps (called buboes—hence the name "bubonic") that could be as big as an apple. An infected person would also experience vomiting, headaches, high fever, extreme pain, possibly delirium, and possibly death. Their chance of dying (in the olden days before treatment) was 30 to 60 percent.

The disease rapidly moved through towns, and bodies piled up. A writer in Florence, Italy, grotesquely compared the mass graves to making lasagna. Churches would dig large pits, and family members would bring their loved ones' bodies and lower them into the ground. Then workers would cover the layer of bodies with a layer of dirt. The next day, more dead would be lowered into the pit, and then another layer of dirt added. On and on it went, bodies and dirt, bodies and dirt, similar to a chef making lasagna with cheese and noodles, cheese and noodles.

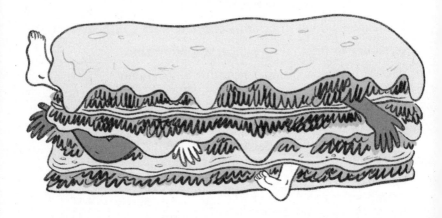

For centuries, no one knew *exactly* why or how the disease spread. While fleas kicked off the plague in a community, body fluids—like blood, mucus, and pus—also passed on the infection. (People sort of knew part of this—that humans could infect humans. That's why the rich ran to their country homes.) Doctors even gave bad advice like "Don't bathe." We now understand germs and know that soap and water (or hand sanitizer) can stop the spread of contagions. Not so in previous centuries, when medical experts thought taking a hot bath would open one's pores and make a person more susceptible to the plague. Many mistakenly thought the disease was airborne.

It wasn't until 1894 that the bacterium was discovered. This was during the most recent plague epidemic, which started in 1860 and lasted nearly a century, killing about 10 million people worldwide. The plague still exists today, but thanks to better hygiene, it's not as widespread, and thanks to antibiotics, it's mostly treatable.

BACTERIA'S BAD RAP

Plenty of bacteria are serial killers. They cause diseases like cholera, pneumonia, Lyme disease, anthrax, diphtheria, and (as mentioned) the plague. However, if we could somehow rid the world of all bacteria, we would also destroy ourselves.

Bacteria have called Earth home for billions of years. They live everywhere: in the ocean, in fresh water, in soil, in animals, in plants, and even, occasionally, in the air. Some thrive at freezing temperatures, while other bacteria love nearly boiling temps. In your body, bacteria outnumber human cells ten to one! Most are harmless, but some are essential. Your gut would not be able to digest food without the help of bacteria. Yep, we need bacteria, just not the pathogen (meaning: disease-causing microorganisms) kind.

SMALLPOX (VIRUS)

Pinpointing the origin of this virus is difficult, maybe impossible. It's believed to be at least 3,000 years old, but perhaps older. The Egyptian pharaoh Ramses V died of the disease in 1157 BCE. We know this because his exhumed, mummified body showed evidence—the telltale pockmarks.

Smallpox is a virus that is spread from human to human. No rats or fleas are necessary. An infection starts flu-like: high fever, headache, body aches, and sometimes vomiting. Just as those symptoms subside after two to five days, blisters appear on the face and limbs. The fever will return, and 30 percent of patients will be dead within a few weeks. The non-deadly cases will recover, and the blisters will scab and dry up. When completely healed, people will have pockmark scars and immunity (meaning: lasting protection from the disease).

Smallpox is one of the deadliest diseases in history. When Europeans traveled to the Americas, they brought it with them. The Indigenous populations had no immunity; their bodies were defenseless against the invading infection. The results were devastating. Over 3 million Aztecs died of smallpox after the Spanish carried over the disease in 1519. The Inca were also infected, and their emperor died from it. Smallpox spread among Native American tribes in the US and First Nations in Canada. This wasn't a one-time event. Smallpox raged for generations.

Even in areas accustomed to outbreaks—where some in

the community likely had immunity—smallpox continued to thrive. In the 1700s, it killed 60 million in Europe. In the 1900s, over 300 million died across the globe.

The cause of smallpox was a mystery for thousands of years. People knew it was contagious, but the idea of a tiny infectious organism—a virus!—wasn't something humans comprehended until the twentieth century. However, astute observers noticed that if someone caught and survived smallpox, they didn't get it again. And in some parts of the world, healers began a practice called variolation. This procedure involved grinding up smallpox victims' scabs and then blowing the dried material into a healthy person's nose. Or another method involved extracting the pus from a smallpox sore and rubbing it into a healthy person's cut. Hopefully, the healthy recipient of these procedures would get only mildly sick and then be immune for the rest of their life. Sadly, 2 to 3 percent of people died from this preventative treatment.

Variolation was not available to everyone; it was mostly limited to the well-off. Then there was the risk of three out of every 100 people dying, which is a terrible mortality rate by modern standards. In 1796, a better solution was discovered. A doctor named Edward Jenner observed that milkmaids (women who milked cows for a living) rarely got smallpox. *Lucky milkmaids!* But it wasn't luck. Milkmaids often contracted cowpox—a hazard of the job—a mild disease transferred from bovine to human. People got blisters from cowpox but ultimately survived. (Cows don't die from it either.) So Jenner decided to try something—something we would consider wildly unethical by twenty-first-century standards.

A milkmaid named Sarah Nelmes had contracted cowpox from a bovine called Blossom. Jenner extracted pus from one of Nelmes's sores. Then he took the pus and purposely infected his gardener's eight-year-old son, James Phipps. Essentially, Jenner gave James a shot of cowpox. The boy was sick in bed for a few days but recovered. Then Jenner exposed James to smallpox. James didn't catch smallpox. Jenner repeated the exposure, and James was always A-OK. He was immune.

The medical rule-makers were not immediately in favor of this new idea, which became known as vaccination. Giving someone a bit of disease to protect them later seemed risky. But Jenner believed in it and went on to vaccinate his infant son. Eventually, scientists realized that vaccines work, and countries began vaccinating their populations against smallpox. In 1934, smallpox outbreaks were a thing of the past in England. In Canada, the disease was last seen in 1946, and it was erased from the US in 1949. About twenty years later, the World Health Organization (WHO) set out to rid the world of smallpox through vaccinations, and by 1980, they announced victory.

Smallpox still lives in labs, and some countries keep vaccines around just in case, but it is considered the first disease that humans eradicated. *Yay for life-saving vaccines!* And it all started with Blossom, Sarah, James, and Dr. Jenner. (While it's now considered unethical to experiment on your gardener's children, Dr. Jenner did buy James's family a house some years later, and James attended Jenner's funeral. Guess they remained friends-*ish*.)

NEW THREATS

Humans have successfully dealt with the plague and smallpox. These are not things we need to worry about anymore. So now that we've cleared some headspace, where should we look for the next mega disease? Let's start with COVID since it's a recent collective memory.

COVID-19 (VIRUS)

COVID-19 is the illness caused by a coronavirus, specifically SARS-CoV-2. It emerged in humans in late 2019. (There have been other human coronaviruses since 2002, including SARS and MERS.) SARS-CoV-2 originated in Wuhan, China, and quickly spread around the world thanks to travel. In March 2020, the World Health Organization declared COVID-19 a pandemic. This is their way of saying, "Yo! This is a planetwide problem. Pay attention and be careful."

Undoubtedly, we have all been affected by COVID-19. Depending on where we live, schools and businesses may have been closed. Fun events we were looking forward to might have been canceled. It may have changed how we shop (stockpile toilet paper), how we dress (masks became fashion accessories), and how we spend our time (home for months). Some of us may have contracted SARS-CoV-2 or may know someone who got sick. Sadly, many people have died from COVID-19. As of mid-2021, over 4.5 million worldwide have died, including more than 664,000 Americans.

The response to this modern pandemic varied across the world. Some nations went into lockdown, not allowing foreigners to visit and putting restrictions on citizens' activities. Other countries tried for "herd immunity" and did not impose safety regulations. They expected most residents—especially young and healthy people—to catch the disease, survive, and then be immune. With herd immunity, the theory is that the coronavirus would run out of potential victims and go away.

The United States COVID-19 response varied from state to state and even from community to community. Initially, in the spring of 2020, New York City was hit hardest, but by the end of the year, other parts of the country experienced high infection rates and devastating loss of life. In January 2021, over 3,000 Americans were dying a day. Containing the virus was an impossibility at this point. Luckily, vaccines were approved by the US government around the same time, but administering the new shots took a while. It was a terrifying race to save lives.

The impact of this disease—which is ongoing as I write this—will be examined in the coming months and years. But looking at the first year of data alone, it appears the United States of America's attempt to stop the spread of COVID-19 ranks among the worst of any nation.

Numbers from March 11, 2021
(one year after WHO declared a pandemic)

Worldwide Infections: 118,357,116

USA Infections: 29,206,727

Worldwide Deaths: 2,625,729

USA Deaths: 530,523

Americans make up only 4.25 percent of the world's population, but on March 11, 2021, Americans made up 20.2 percent of the world's deaths due to coronavirus.

Scientists and researchers will have to figure out how a wealthy and scientifically advanced country was so unprepared. And more important, they will need to determine how every nation can stop outbreaks in the future.

FLU (VIRUS)

This annual problem returns every fall and winter. Not because the flu likes cold weather but because humans hang out inside more when the weather gets chilly. This respiratory virus is easily spread in the warm indoor air. A good, uncovered sneeze can spray droplets across a room.

The flu causes *flu-like* symptoms, obviously. Some specifics: fever, body aches, cough, and other lung-related problems. In severe cases, the flu can kill and usually targets very young children, older adults, and people who have other illnesses. Yet it has killed healthy adults and kids too. On average, 12,000 to 61,000 flu deaths happen in the USA annually. There are seasonal vaccines for the flu but no cure.

EBOLA (VIRUS)

This is a rare but scary virus that affects humans, other primates, and, occasionally, pigs. It originated in Africa and caught the world's attention because it's an awful and deadly disease. The symptoms include fever, rash, and then major hemorrhaging (meaning: a large amount of uncontrolled bleeding). And that blood is coming from every hole in the body. Ebola is a big-time killer. Anywhere between 25 and 90 percent of Ebola victims will die, depending on the strand of the virus. The 2014–2016 Ebola epidemic resulted in 11,325 deaths, mostly in West Africa. Humans catch Ebola from infected body fluids like blood and saliva. There's no vaccine or cure.

MALARIA (PARASITE)

This potentially deadly parasite (not a virus or bacterium) is transmitted to humans by *Anopheles* mosquitoes. It's common in tropical regions, and symptoms are similar to the flu: fever, body aches, chills, headache, and sometimes diarrhea and vomiting. In 2008, approximately 228 million were infected, and 405,000 died. Often, it's children who experience the worst of it. Vaccines are being tried, and some treatments are available, but we don't have a cure.

SUPERBUGS

In 1928, scientist Alexander Fleming noticed his bacteria sample died when it was accidentally exposed to a mold. From this *oops* moment, the world's first antibiotic was born. Initially, Fleming called it "mould juice" before renaming it penicillin in honor of the mold. An injectable form became available in 1941, which was very useful in World War II.

Before antibiotics, a small cut could kill, surgeries were incredibly risky, and childbirth posed a threat to mom and baby. All because of the chance of bacterial infection. Antibiotics can also treat bacteria-borne diseases like strep throat, whooping cough, scarlet fever, pneumonia, anthrax, syphilis, typhus, and the plague. (Antibiotics are useless against a virus.) Life expectancy in the United States went from sixty-eight years old in 1950 to seventy-eight years old in 2016, partly thanks to the golden age of antibiotics.

But now it seems bacteria are fighting back against our human ingenuity. Superbugs are germs (bacteria or fungi) that are super resistant to the medicines designed to destroy them. According to a recent report, the US sees over 2.8 million antibiotic-resistant infections annually, which leads to 35,000 American deaths. Superbugs are developing faster than we can find new treatments. In 2019, the Centers for Disease Control and Prevention (CDC) had eighteen bacteria and fungi on their super-bug threat list. One is known as "nightmare bacteria," and some varieties are immune to nearly all antibiotics.

100 PERCENT DEADLY

Good news. We currently don't have an infectious disease that is 100 percent fatal. But we do have plenty of viruses, bacteria, and parasites that can wipe out large portions of the population. We need to develop universal vaccines—like something that'll take care of all flu strands so we don't need a new shot every school year. And we need treatments, cures, and vaccines available around the world, not just in places with drugstores and internet access. However, there's always a chance an old disease will mutate, or a new organism will emerge that's an efficient mass murderer. No doubt, scientists will continue the battle to keep our species alive and healthy.

CHAPTER 9
OVERPOPULATION
WE LIVE HERE, WE EAT HERE—
UNTIL WE DON'T!

Currently, there are 7.9 billion–ish people on Earth. And that's including the handful of people orbiting the planet on the International Space Station.

In 1500, right around the time the first Europeans sailed to the Americas, the world's population was approximately 450 million people. (That's about the same number of people in the USA and Mexico today.) In 1804, Earth crossed the 1-billion-human-inhabitants line. Are you doing the math? That was, like, 300,000 years to hit nearly half a billion and then a mere 300 years to double the world's population.

And things only sped up from there. In 1927, Earth was home to 2 billion. In 1960, 3 billion. In 1999, 6 billion. In 2011, 7 billion. We'll cross 8 billion by 2025. This is wild, exciting growth, and it's best illustrated in a GIF, but since books can't do that yet, a graph will have to do. (See next page.)

Basically, Earth has a major human infestation problem. Well, is it a problem? While the planet is mostly water, there's still plenty of land—about 57 million square miles. If we all

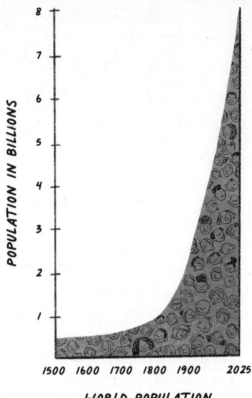

WORLD POPULATION

moved to Africa—where our species is from—we could each have slightly less than an acre to call our own. (That's nearly three-quarters of a football field.) Of course, not all the land is ideal for setting up a home. Deserts, swamps, and barren rocks are not prime real estate. But still, Earth offers plenty of space for our expanding population.

The issue is that humans don't just need a place to live. We want room for everything from schools to stores to factories to landfills to the biggest gobbler of real estate, agriculture.

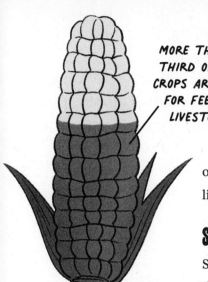

MORE THAN A THIRD OF OUR CROPS ARE USED FOR FEEDING LIVESTOCK.

About 50 percent of Earth's habitable land (meaning: areas not barren or covered by glaciers) is used for farming, and most of that is for raising and feeding livestock.

SAD

SAD is an acronym for "standard American diet." It's a generalization about eating habits in the United States, where meals tend to have large portions of meat and other animal products, like eggs and cheese. Statistics show that the average American consumes a whopping 222 pounds of red meat and poultry per year. For each person who partakes in the standard American diet, 2.67 acres of land (or about two football fields) are needed to grow and raise that food per year.

Sample SAD menu

eggs and bacon for breakfast

cheeseburger for lunch

spaghetti and meatballs for dinner

If every human ate this way, we would need two planet

Earths to grow and raise enough food. As of the printing of this book, there's only one planet Earth.

Luckily for our farmland and our cows, the standard American diet is not the standard earthling diet. Meal plans that center on fruits, vegetables, and grains need less land. They're also healthier.

Unluckily for us, the world's population is growing. More mouths to feed! We aren't out of food yet (or the land needed to create food), but we also do not have the balance we need for long-term health.

ONE POUND OF MEAT REQUIRES
260 SQUARE FEET OF FARMLAND.

H_2O

Humans can continue to eat at Earth's buffet as long as everyone doesn't chow down on steak and bacon daily. But what about that other basic need? Water—or more accurately, clean water. Unsafe H_2O can contain disease-spreading microscopic organisms or other harmful elements.

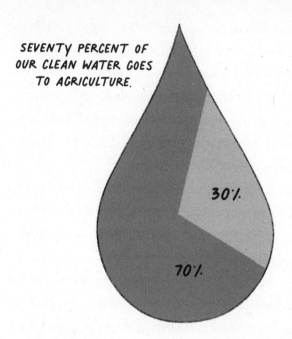

SEVENTY PERCENT OF OUR CLEAN WATER GOES TO AGRICULTURE.

30%

70%

Technically, Earth has plenty of clean drinking water for all its humans. Even as our population increases to 10 billion over the next few decades, we should still have enough. Yet there are already 2.1 billion people who do not have safe drinking water at home. That's about one in four people. Some places physically do not have water, and some areas do not have the infrastructure (pipes and such) to distribute water. Water scarcity is a problem on every continent.

Let's look at the water crisis in Mexico City, which is home to more than 21 million people. Even though the city gets enough rain, most water runs into the sewer and is not collected for human use. Mexico City gets half of its clean water from aquifers, but they are being drained faster than the water can naturally be replaced. Also, about 40 percent of clean water is lost due to leaky pipes throughout the city. The lowest-income neighborhoods have it hardest. In the areas with no water or sewage infrastructure, water has to be brought in by trucks. And things are getting worse! By 2050, scientists believe Mexico City will have 10 to 17 percent less natural water because of climate change.

The United States has seen a different kind of water crisis in Flint, Michigan. For decades, the city got its water from nearby Detroit. Then, in 2014, Flint city officials had a money-saving idea. *We have a river—the Flint River—so let's use that to supply our water instead of paying Detroit.* But soon after the city switched water sources, residents noticed a funny metallic taste and, a little later, a change in color. (Personally, I don't want my water to have any color!) A scandal and a mystery followed. The scandal was that officials declared the water safe. It certainly was not. The water contained high amounts of lead, which causes cancer and developmental delays in children. (There were other nasty ingredients in the water, but lead was the biggest problem.) The mystery was, why was this happening? The Flint River did not have high levels of lead. The problem turned out to be the city's old pipes, which were made of iron and lead, and the Flint River water was not being treated with anticorrosive agents like the Detroit water had been. The pipes, both under the city and in homes, polluted the water. In November 2015, Flint switched back to Detroit water, but the damage was already done to the water lines and people's confidence in Flint's H_2O. Many residents still use bottled water, an expensive alternative to tap water.

So how much water do we need? The average adult man needs to drink about one gallon per day, but H_2O is more than a refreshing beverage. In the US, a single person can use about 100 gallons per day. That's water for baths, showers, cooking, laundry, toilets, brushing teeth and other hygiene, and drinking. The World Health Organization would like to see every human have access to at least thirteen to twenty-six gallons of water per day. When Cape Town in South Africa experienced shortages in 2018, each person was limited to thirteen gallons per day. (Hey, that's the minimum of the minimum!) In Mexico City, residents with the lowest incomes are surviving on five gallons per day.

PACKING 'EM IN

The United Nations (UN) predicts that the human population will hit nearly 10 billion around 2050. (Technically, they say 9.7 billion.) But *Homo sapiens* will not be spread evenly around the globe. Europe's and North America's numbers are projected to increase until 2042, and then they'll likely drop. Central and southern Asia's populations will continue to grow, and sub-Saharan Africa's will boom. But again, humans will not be spread out evenly across a continent or even a country. People like to congregate in cities. We are social animals!

Overcrowding in urban areas can strain public services like water, electricity, sanitation (toilets and such), and our favorite, the internet. Crowding also makes disease more rampant—as we saw in the last chapter. If you've ever been in a class where one kid gets the stomach bug, and by the end of the week, half the kids are throwing up and probably the teacher too, you've seen a micro example of how illnesses can spread when people are in very close contact. Or maybe you've witnessed an outbreak of lice. This happens in cities too, not just kindergarten classrooms. (Life tip: Never share hats or hair scrunchies.)

It's not just human-to-human contact that can cause problems with disease. In 1854, more than 600 people in a London neighborhood died from cholera within a ten-day period. A doctor determined that the culprit was the contaminated Broad Street water pump used by most of the community. A typhus outbreak hit Los Angeles, California, in 2018. The bacteria-driven disease is spread by fleas and has been called "jail fever" and "camp fever" (referring to something like an internment or refugee camp, not a summer camp). Typhus thrives in overcrowded, less sanitary areas. The LA outbreak was centered around a homeless community. If diseases and infections could talk, they'd probably say, "The more, the merrier," when it comes to packing humans into small areas.

LIMITED RESOURCES

You may have noticed that Earth imports few resources from other planets or solar systems. Sure, we get heat, light, and energy from the sun (which is responsible for the growth of *everything* on the planet), but we don't get food from Mars, or water from Jupiter, or sneakers from Mercury. Everything humans need must come from our home planet, and these resources have limits.

Some resources do not replenish—for example, fossil fuels. We have a finite supply of the coal, oil, and natural gas found deep in the ground. No elves are making more. Other resources like timber, food, and fresh water are renewable—though not by elves either. However, humans are using these resources faster than they are replenished. It's estimated we are currently consuming the resources of 1.7 Earths. Or, to say it another way, we need 1.7 planet Earths to enjoy our current lifestyle in the long run. Let's look at it like this. Imagine our planet has a giant warehouse of all the food, water, and materials we need. What's in that warehouse needs to last us—all of humanity—an entire year. Well, in 2019, we emptied the warehouse on July 29. The rest of the year, we were "borrowing" from future warehouses. This deficit cannot be sustained. (In 2020, the empty-the-warehouse date—more commonly known as Earth Overshoot Day—was August 22. This improvement was probably due to our pandemic lifestyle and not humankind's decision to use resources more wisely.)

Using the resources of 1.7 Earths to feed and care for one Earth is bad, but rich nations (see note below) like the United States consume even more. It's estimated that if the rest of the world lived the *typical* American lifestyle—if all humans ate like Americans, used energy like Americans, shopped like Americans—we'd need the producing power of five Earths. We'd have to recruit Mercury, Venus, Mars, our moon, and probably Pluto to grow vegetables, raise cattle, and make T-shirts.

IMPORTANT NOTE!

The United States is often referred to as a "rich nation." But what does that mean? One way to measure a nation's wealth is to take the country's income (the money earned by all people and businesses, domestically and from abroad) and divide it by the number of citizens. This is called the gross national income per capita (or GNI per capita). Mathematically, it looks like this.

GNI per Capita = All the Income ÷ All the People

For the United States, that number was $65,850 in 2019. The world's average was $11,571. Based on GNI per capita, the USA is one of the ten wealthiest countries. HOWEVER (that's in all caps on purpose), America has the highest income inequality of the top twenty-five nations. The fifty richest Americans have more money than the lowest-earning half of US citizens. Over 1.3 million students in public schools were homeless for at least part of the 2016–2017 school year. That's 3 percent of students. Approximately 13 million American children face food insecurity (meaning: a lack of food on a consistent basis). That's one out of six kids!

Okay, enough with the numbers. Simply put, we can call the USA a rich nation. But we can also call it a nation of inequality and a nation with a significant poverty issue.

ANIMALS WE'VE WIPED OFF THE FACE OF THE EARTH

Generally speaking, *Homo sapiens* are not cannibals. There are a few notorious exceptions, but we are not likely to go extinct from eating each other. However, we *have* eaten other species into oblivion.

For most of human history, scholars did not accept the concept of extinction. Some thought the idea went against God or the power of Mother Nature. In 1818, Thomas Jefferson even wrote, "It might be doubted whether any particular species of animals or vegetables, which ever did exist, has ceased to exist." The extinction debate raged for decades, but it is now undeniable. We know that plenty of animals—like all the non-avian dinosaurs—have been wiped out. Actually, most animals. (It's worth repeating that approximately 99 percent of all species to ever exist are now gone.)

Anthropologists have been able to trace the demise of megafauna (meaning: giant animals) to the expansion of *Homo sapiens* across the globe. Fifty thousand years ago, mammoths lived on every continent except Australia and Antarctica. Not all the mammoths were the woolly kind we know from cavemen cartoons. That breed dominated in northern climates. Wherever humans traveled, they ate these elephant relatives—both the woolly and non-woolly kinds. Before the arrival of humans, mammoths didn't have predators. Then, all of a sudden, spear-wielding, two-legged animals show up and light the barbecue. Other factors, like changing climates, may have helped drive the mammoth to extinction, but we cannot overlook the role of humans' appetites.

A more recent—and much smaller—animal we ate into oblivion is the passenger pigeon, which is ironic because, in 1796, this bird saved colonists from starvation after a crop failure. Two hundred years ago, this "pigeon-sized pigeon" was abundant in North America. They numbered in the billions and probably made up 40 percent of the total bird population on the continent. In 1833, John James Audubon (a naturalist and famous bird painter) noted mile-wide flocks blocking out the sun for days and described the birds' dung falling like melting snow. *Gross!* Passenger pigeons were easy to hunt because they traveled in huge numbers. A single gunshot could kill several birds. But hunters didn't need guns; they could toss nets into the sky to snag the pigeons. No net? One man in San Antonio reportedly killed over 400 by whacking them with a small stick.

The tasty bird was sold on the cheap in town markets and served in fancy restaurants and lowly roadside taverns (the fast-food establishments of the day). It could be used in many recipes; a popu-lar dish was passenger pigeon pot pie, which was sometimes served with pigeon feet stick-ing out of the crust.

Overhunting of these birds eventually led to their demise. With the advancement of the telegraph, professional hunters could communicate the locations of the huge flocks. And with the improvements to the railroad, hunters could quickly travel to the roosting sites. The trains were also helpful for shipping dead birds by the barrel across the country. (The pigeon also suffered from habitat loss at the hands of humans.) Once their numbers diminished, the birds became vulnerable to other predators. The passenger pigeon became extinct in the wild in the mid-1890s.

We can no longer munch on passenger pigeons, but we can observe a dead one. Martha, the last of her species, died in captivity on September 1, 1914. Her body is on display in the Smithsonian in Washington, DC.

GROWING, GROWING, GROWN

Our growing population is more of a problem for all the other species on the planet than for *Homo sapiens*. Our exploding numbers will not lead to our extinction, obviously. But as a species, we should consider the quality of life of every member of our human family. Do we have enough food, fresh water, clean air, and safe habitats for 10 billion or 11 billion people? Can we offer medical treatment to everyone?

And is it our job to consider other species? Or is it every critter for itself? Certainly, other animals aren't forward-thinking. A lion doesn't wonder if she's eating the last gazelle or if there will be more gazelles to eat next week. But our advanced brains and reasoning allow us to examine the future. Our gray matter also gives us the ability to abuse and destroy everything around us. As humans, we get to decide how we treat Earth and *all* its species—the species we plan on eating and even the ones we don't.

CHAPTER 10
WAR
THE ULTIMATE SELF-DESTRUCT BUTTON

Humans are good at killing each other. As mentioned in previous chapters, it's possible (likely) that *Homo sapiens* destroyed other humans, and early nomadic *H. sapiens* probably fought each other for resources. Once humans formed settlements, things got serious. Non-nomadic humans had more stuff to protect, like homes and land and electronics, not to mention weapons were getting more advanced.

War! Commonly defined as conflicts between states or nations—or sometimes within countries, AKA civil war. Our first battle records are carved in stones dating back to 2700 BCE. These tablets document a conflict between Sumerians and Elamites in the Middle East. And somewhere in the world, humans have seemingly been fighting each other ever since.

THINGS GO NUCLEAR

Through the centuries, wars have gone from up close and personal, fought with weapons like spears, to distant and destructive, using bombs and the vehicles needed to deliver them. But things got intense—and terrifying—with the invention of the nuclear bomb.

In 1939, German scientists discovered fission. Simply put, fission is the splitting of an atom. This process, which releases a ton of energy, is how nuclear power plants generate electricity and is the reason that nuclear bombs are so destructive. When other scientists learned of this German accomplishment, the world got nervous. If Germany got their hands on the right materials, Hitler's government could build the world's first nuclear bomb. So physicists Albert Einstein and Leo Szilard decided to text President Roosevelt. Kidding. They knew about fission but not cell phones; they sent a letter. This prompted the president to start the Advisory Committee on Uranium—a key ingredient in nuclear bomb making.

In February 1940, with a starting budget of $6,000, research began in the United States. Much of the early work happened at Columbia University in Manhattan. As this secret work spread to scientists and institutions across the country, it earned the code name the Manhattan Project. Thousands of Americans developed the first nuclear bomb, and most involved didn't know what they were part of. They simply knew it was a war effort. Even in Congress (the folks in charge of funding), most members were kept in the dark about the project's ultimate goal.

Fun fact: Einstein never worked on the Manhattan Project. He did not have the military clearance needed and couldn't get it because he was an outspoken pacifist.

FUTURE NUCLEAR PHYSICISTS! HERE'S WHAT YOU NEED TO KNOW

The atom is the smallest form of matter. At its center, an atom has a nucleus composed of protons and neutrons (except for hydrogen, which has no neutrons). Zooming around the nucleus are electrons. A hydrogen atom has one proton and one electron. A helium atom has two protons and two electrons. (Check out a periodic table for more elements.)

Fission—Atoms Splitting Apart

- Occurs when a neutron slams into an atom and divides it into two new atoms.

- Releases huge amounts of energy.

- Plutonium and uranium are the elements often used for this reaction.

- Nuclear power plants are fission-driven.

- Weapons that use fission reactions are often called atomic bombs.

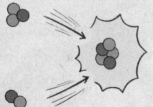

Fusion—Atoms Coming Together

- Occurs when two atoms slam into each other and make a new atom. Like when two hydrogen atoms join to create a helium atom.

- Releases a ginormous amount of energy— several times more than a fission reaction.

- The sun is driven by fusion.

- Weapons that use fusion reactions are often called thermonuclear or hydrogen bombs.

The first test of a nuclear bomb (code name: Trinity) took place on July 16, 1945, in New Mexico. This prototype wasn't dropped from the air. Instead, scientists placed the bomb, nicknamed Gadget, on a radio tower in the middle of the desert. Before this device was detonated, all proposed outcomes were purely theoretical. They were just best-guess calculations. The scientists were reasonably confident the nuclear bomb would not melt our atmosphere or evaporate our oceans. The chances of that happening were very, very small. Because of their uncertainty, the scientists thought it would be fun to bet on the destructive power of Trinity. For a mere dollar entry fee, these brilliant minds guessed at the explosive force. The official estimate for the Trinity test was a range of 500 to 7,000 tons of TNT. (The power of a bomb is measured in how much TNT we would need to create an equivalent explosion.) In pre-nuclear 1945, the biggest bomb the US had was equal to only ten tons of TNT.

So what was Trinity's explosivity? Drum roll, please. *Tat-tat-tat-tat.* Trinity achieved nearly 21,000 tons of TNT destructiveness. On one July day, humanity multiplied its bombing power by 2,000.

On August 6, 1945, less than a month after the Trinity test, the United States dropped a nuclear bomb on Hiroshima, Japan, killing 70,000 instantly. Three days later, the US hit

Nagasaki, killing another 40,000. Many others died in the days, weeks, and months after the bombings. On August 15, a radio message was broadcast across Japan from the emperor, announcing the country's surrender. World War II formally ended a few weeks later, on September 2.

The American bombing of Hiroshima and Nagasaki is the only time in history that nuclear weapons have been used against people. (There have been plenty of tests.) The decision to drop atomic bombs would later be questioned and criticized by historians. At this point in World War II, Germany and Italy were done. The Allies had only Japan to deal with, and the Japanese military was not at its peak. Even without "Little Boy" and "Fat Man" (those were the bombs' names), the US would likely have defeated Japan. But it probably would have taken months and cost the lives of thousands of US soldiers and Marines. At the time, much of the world was convinced that every last Japanese citizen—including the children—would fight to save their empire.

Another theory speculates that the US decided to hit Japan with nuclear force because the Manhattan Project was expensive. Why spend all that money on a mega weapon that never gets used?

President Truman was the man who'd ultimately been in charge of deciding whether to use (or not use) nuclear weapons on American enemies. Yet he didn't even know about the Manhattan Project until April 12, 1945, after President Roosevelt died and Truman took the oath of office. We can imagine the secretary of war tapping him on the shoulder and saying, "By the way, we're working on this fission-driven weapon that might destroy humanity." Even before the successful Trinity test in July, Truman put together a committee to decide if and where the atomic bomb should be used—basically, could it be used to end the war? The committee suggested dropping a nuclear bomb on Japan without warning. Americans were tired of war and had recently experienced Japan's strength and determination on Okinawa. It took twelve weeks for the US to take control of the island, and it cost 50,000 American lives. (Japan suffered even greater casualties than the US: 90,000 troops and 100,000 civilians.)

Records indicate that there was some discussion of just showing off America's nuclear bomb—dropping a nuke on some uninhabited island and allowing the world to watch. But officials worried a demonstration might not have had the same persuasive power. Plus, the US had only two atomic bombs at this time, and using one for show might have been considered wasteful.

The site of Hiroshima was selected because of its military importance (an army headquarters) and industrial capabilities (factories). Also, it was a compact city with neighboring hills, which would "considerably increase the blast damage," according to US government target committee meetings. Prior to August 6, 1945, Hiroshima had not endured an Allied attack. It was a blank slate. Scientists and the military would be able to review before-and-after photos (and other data) to see how a nuclear bomb destroyed a city.

The death toll at Hiroshima was astounding. But it was not the worst the Japanese people endured. The three-hour fire-bombing of Tokyo in March 1945 killed approximately 100,000 people. In Operation Meetinghouse, the US Army Air Forces used 300 B-29 bombers to drop 1,500 tons of firebombs on Tokyo, burning over sixteen square miles. It was the deadliest air raid in history—more fatal than Hiroshima or Nagasaki.

But Little Boy and Fat Man didn't require 300 planes. The attacks on Hiroshima and Nagasaki each required only one bomb and one aircraft. And, in 1945, only the Americans had the science and technology to deliver that destruction.

This next section is horrific and sad. I considered leaving out the details about Hiroshima and Nagasaki but decided that a discussion of nuclear horrors is important to understanding our destructive capabilities. *Humans did this to humans!* If you're even slightly uncomfortable, please skip ahead to the next section: "Brrr! A Cold War." You can always come back when you're ready.

HOW NUCLEAR IS DIFFERENT

Let's talk about the destructive power of nuclear weapons. Little Boy and Fat Man killed hundreds of thousands of Japanese people. Many more were injured and lost their homes. Thousands of children became *genbaku-koji* (translation: atomic bomb orphans). Because some people survived these bombings, we have firsthand accounts of this human-caused tragedy. And while the following is hard to read, I feel it's essential that we do not ignore the awful consequences experienced in Hiroshima and Nagasaki. Perish the thought that someday, someone could again be deciding if a nuclear bomb should be used on people. Casualties are easily summed up in numbers, but the details of the devastation are much harder to forget or ignore. Another warning before you read on: This is horrific and sad.

During the war, Japanese citizens were accustomed to listening for planes and air-raid sirens. Many survivors describe hearing the plane on August 6, and a few were close enough to see a black dot in the sky—Little Boy being dropped. Then there was the flash of light. The bomb ignited 1,900 feet above the ground and appeared brighter than the sun. Some people had a moment to drop to the ground or get under a table. There wasn't time for much else. Anyone in the immediate area was instantly killed. The explosion was so intense that the remains of many of the victims were never recovered.

After the bright light came the blast of heat and air; this

was powerful enough to knock over people and buildings. Across the city, glass shattered. Those turned toward the bright light suffered flash burns on their faces and other exposed skin on the fronts of their bodies. Those who turned away were burned on their backs. These burns were not charred like we might imagine from a flame; instead, the victims' skin melted off, leaving exposed flesh. Faces became unrecognizable. One survivor recalls his friend's face swollen to three times its size with skin melting away. One doctor describes victims as walking like scarecrows with arms outstretched because the pain from burns on their arms was so intense they could not rest their limbs against their torsos.

These new bombs dropped on Japan did not just kill with severe burns and blast wounds. People in Hiroshima and Nagasaki were exposed to dangerous radiation. For some, it caused bleeding gums and intense vomiting. Blisters formed on the outside *and* on the inside of the body. Organs turned black and shut down. Radiation victims often died a slow, painful death over days or weeks.

The effects of the bombs did not end with the war but lasted years. One woman describes picking glass out of her skin a decade later. The small pieces were driven so deep into her body that they took years to "grow out." Some survivors experienced lifelong health problems and higher cancer rates. Scientists are still trying to determine if the radiation exposure experienced by survivors could even have had an impact on the health of their future children.

A nuclear bomb's ability to kill and harm is like nothing humanity has ever seen. And while the atomic bombing of Hiroshima and Nagasaki ended World War II, a hot second later, a new kind of war started. Welcome to the Cold War and the arms race.

BRRR! A COLD WAR

While the United States developed the first nuclear bomb, other nations were not far behind. By 1960, England, France, and the USSR had their own big bombs. And not only that, the technology was getting better. (*Better?* If more destructive power is better, then yes, that's the right word.) Scientists first used fission (breaking atoms apart) for nuclear weapons, but they soon learned they could get even more energy by putting atoms together. Fusion!

Since fission bombs were soooo last year, world superpowers began making the fusion kind. And in October 1961, the USSR tested the largest bomb ever on Novaya Zemlya, an archipelago in the Arctic Ocean. Tsar Bomba—also known as Big Ivan—measured a yield of fifty megatons of TNT, which is 3,800 times more powerful than Little Boy. Big Ivan was truly a *big boy* at twenty-six feet long, weighing twenty-seven tons. That's nearly three times heavier than the biggest *T. rex* ever found.

Over the next decades, nations (especially the United States and the USSR) would spend billions of dollars building the biggest bombs and the cleverest systems for delivering them. Warheads! Humans could now put nuclear weapons in the tip of a ballistic missile and fire at each other from far away. At the height of the Cold War, an estimated 70,000 nuclear warheads were stockpiled worldwide. In 2021, that number was cut back to 13,100, thanks to treaties and global agreements.

ENOUGH FOR HUMAN EXTINCTION?

Even though the worldwide nuclear stockpile is less than it was at its prime, are there enough bombs to wipe out our own existence? Simple answer: probably not. We do not have the military might to blow up the planet literally. Earth itself is safe. If we wanted to (*and why would we want to?*), we could wipe out a significant amount of our population by strategically placing all our nuclear devices across the globe. There are certainly enough weapons to take out all the cities, towns, and villages. But still, over 3 billion people live in rural areas. It would be impossible to reach everyone. (*And again, why would we want to?*) However, the nuclear winter that would follow—freezing temperatures, high levels of radiation, crop failure, contaminated water—just might erase the rest of Earth's *Homo sapiens* population.

The sheer number of nuclear weapons we have is impressive and appalling. Every human on this planet is the same species and shares 99.9 percent of the same DNA. We are all related. The idea that we can wipe out millions of our relatives with the push of a button is terrifying. (I jest, calling nuclear detonation a simple button, but the decision to strike does rest in the hands of just a few leaders.) While these weapons have not been used against people since 1945 and things have calmed down since the height of the Cold War, we live with the possibility that that might change any day. We cannot control an asteroid strike or a volcanic eruption, but nuclear war starts and ends with us.

Nagasaki survivor Inosuke Hayasaki put it beautifully: "The ability to live in peace is a country's most prized commodity."

CHAPTER 11

SUN

WE'RE GONNA NEED STRONGER SPF

While every other apocalyptic ending we've discussed is theoretically possible, the collapse of our sun is a guarantee. Our sun is a G2 V, AKA a yellow dwarf. It was born about 4.6 billion years ago, probably spawned from the energy of another star dying. Yellow dwarf stars are ideal from our point of view, because they're pretty reliable. Their heat, light, and size change slowly and predictably. (Unlike, say, a blue hypergiant, which is a moody beast that swells and shrinks erratically.) Our sun is basically at its midlife point, which is its most stable point. We expect it to last a total of around 10 billion years. But don't get too comfortable thinking we have another 5 billion years of solar bliss. We have a fraction of that time.

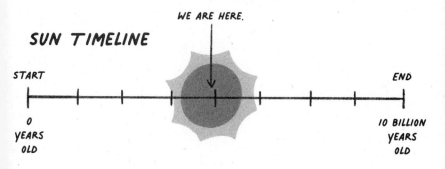

SUN TIMELINE

WE ARE HERE.

START

END

0
YEARS
OLD

10 BILLION
YEARS
OLD

SCIENCE STUFF

At the sun's surface, the temperature is about 10,000°F (5,500°C), and at the center, it's 27,000,000°F (15,000,000°C). The volume of our favorite star is 1.3 million times larger than Earth. If we weighed our entire solar system, the sun would be the bulk of it—99.8 percent. The planets, moons, asteroids, and other stuff are pretty insignificant weight-wise.

Like Earth, the sun rotates. Unlike Earth, the sun does not have solid tectonic plates. So as the sun turns, its surface moves at different speeds. The middle spins faster than the top and bottom, creating a swirly mess. Then, approximately every eleven years, the sun's north pole and south pole flip, and we get a super-active phase called a solar maximum. The result is a surge in solar eruptions and solar flares (meaning: destructive, beautiful bursts of light that shoot from the sun). *Yikes!* Luckily, our atmosphere and magnetic poles keep earthlings safe from these rays. The next solar maximum should be in the summer of 2025.

The sun is powered by hydrogen, which turns into helium thanks to fusion. (Remember fusion from the last chapter?) There's enough hydrogen to satisfy our star's appetite for 3.5 billion more years. When it runs out, the core will be dead, and the sun will swell. It will burn hotter and brighter and expand to become a red giant.

Is this when earthlings will be in trouble? Nope. We have even less than 3.5 billion years before problems ensue.

STABILITY IS IMPORTANT

As mentioned, our sun is a stable yellow dwarf star, which is nice for us. That's not to say it never changes (it totally does!), and those changes can affect life on Earth. Between 1645 and 1715, our star went through a calming phase, which might sound lovely but isn't. Astronomers observed significantly fewer sunspots (meaning: dark, cooler areas on the surface) than in the past. They've named this period the Maunder Minimum, and it wasn't just frustrating to the sun gazers; it may have been responsible for a mini ice age in the northern hemisphere. Things got brutally chilly in the American colonies. The Thames in London froze, as did the canals in Venice. In Iceland and Greenland, fishing villages were abandoned. Glaciers moved over farmland in Norway. Life was harsh. Small changes in the sun can have dramatic impacts on Earth.

It's normal for sunspot activity to increase and decrease during phases of the eleven-year solar cycle, but the Maunder Minimum was unquestionably different and is still unexplained by science.

AND BIG CHANGE IS COMING

In 1 billion years, the sun will be 10 percent brighter. What's that going to look like for Earth? *Hot! Apocalyptically hot!* Earth's water will evaporate, except perhaps what's deep in the ground. All this H_2O in the atmosphere will only make things worse by trapping even more heat. Temperatures will eventually stabilize around 700°F (371°C). That's hotter than any setting on a standard kitchen oven. Except (perhaps) for some organisms deep in Earth's crust, all life will be destroyed.

Humans cannot live on a 700°F planet, no matter how many air conditioners we have running. We need a home in what astrobiologists call the Goldilocks zone—not too close to a star that the planet is burning hot and not too far that it's freezing cold. It has to be just right. (Get it? Goldilocks?) As the sun gets brighter, our local Goldilocks zone will move outward in the solar system. This might make Mars an ideal new home. At least for a while.

The sun will continue to heat up, and when it runs out of hydrogen at the core, it will grow. Not only will it be hotter and brighter, but the star will also swell. It'll balloon beyond the orbits of Mercury and Venus. (Yep, Mercury and Venus will be gobbled up by the sun.) Earth's destiny is up for debate. Scientists agree the planet will be hot (even hotter than 700°F), without liquid water, and void of life, but will the sun swallow our homeland? Maybe. Or Earth's orbit may be nudged farther out into space. The planet might even be knocked out of orbit completely. Luckily, no one will be living here anymore.

Our new home on Mars will no longer be ideal when there's a red giant at the solar system's center. Humans, again, will need to look for new real estate. Possible contenders include dwarf planets Eris and Pluto. *Yes, Pluto!* Scientists

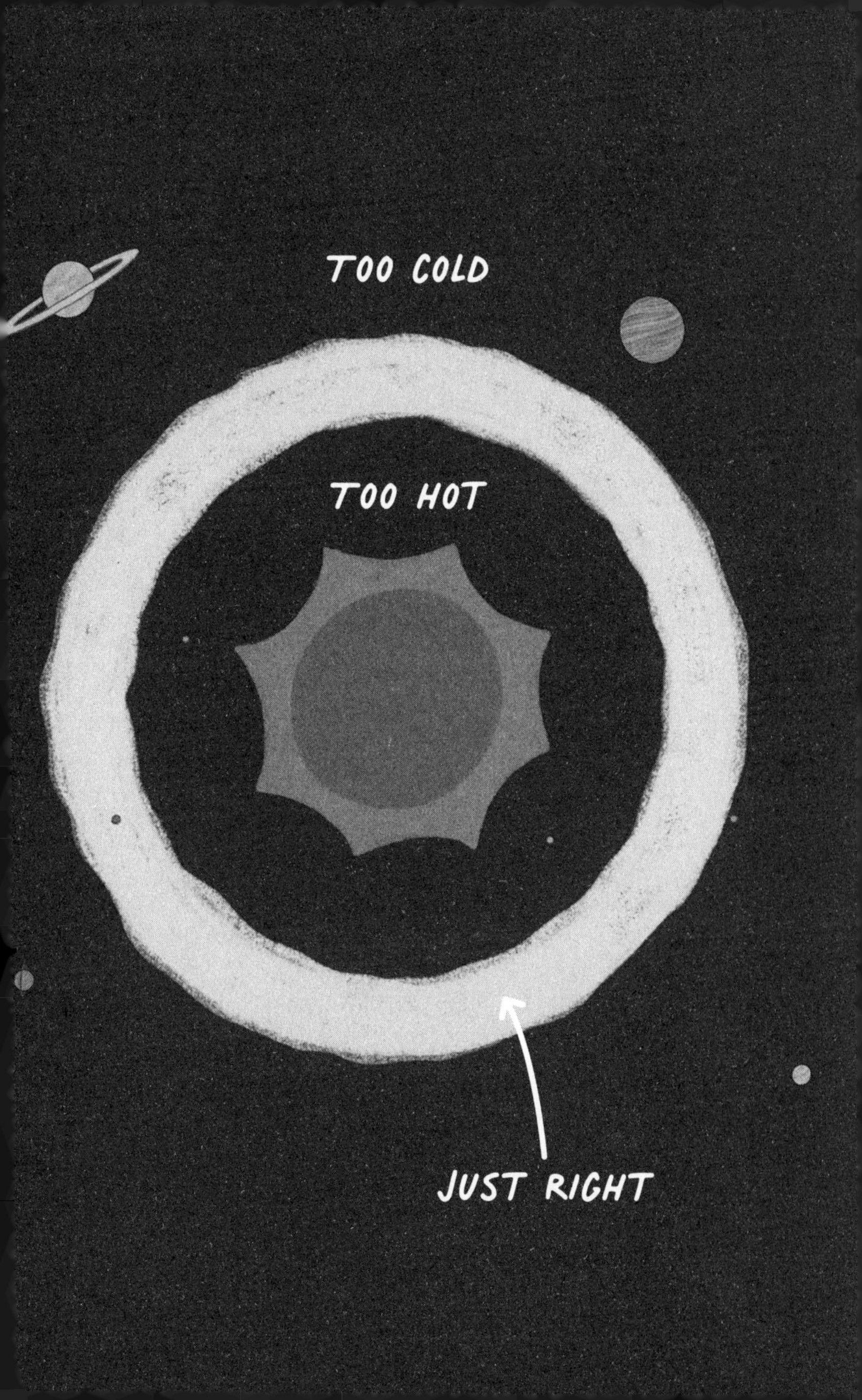
TOO COLD
TOO HOT
JUST RIGHT

and nonscientists love to debate whether Pluto is a planet or a dwarf planet. But our far-in-the-future descendants won't care about titles. They'll just need a cozy home.

Our sun will not maintain this red giant phase forever. As it runs out of fuel on its surface, the sun will shrink down to about the size of Earth, and it'll become a white dwarf, which is a super-dense star. A teaspoon of a white dwarf would weigh about fifteen tons. That's like two African elephants. This ultra-hot star will cool down over the next 100 trillion years until its final stage—black dwarf. (Our sun is too small to create a supernova. More on this in the next chapter.) The sun will still be the size of Earth and incredibly dense, but it will be cold and dark. Today, no black dwarf stars exist. It takes a white dwarf trillions of years to cool off, and the universe is only 13 billion years old. No star is old enough to be a black dwarf yet.

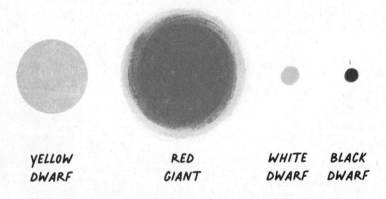

YELLOW DWARF   RED GIANT   WHITE DWARF   BLACK DWARF

Humans living on Pluto or Eris will be packing their bags again before the sun becomes a white dwarf. It'll be time to get out of our solar system. But where to go? Luckily, there might be as many as 300 million habitable planets in the Milky Way. Researchers used data from NASA's Kepler mission to estimate the number of Earth-sized, rocky (not gas!) planets orbiting in the Goldilocks zone around stable, sun-like stars. *Ain't any ole planet gonna do.* Of course, these are just calculations, and a future home planet has not yet been identified. Astronomers have at least a billion years to continue looking.

CORONAL MASS EJECTIONS

While we have plenty of time before Earth becomes a pizza oven, the sun does pose other threats, such as coronal mass ejections (CMEs). These are different from solar flares, but they can occur at the same time. A *Scientific American* article equated sun flares to lightning and CMEs to hurricanes. Both are massive explosions of energy on the sun's surface, but flares are flashes of light and take about eight minutes to get to Earth. CMEs are clouds of burning hot and electrically charged gas (AKA: plasma) and can take fifteen hours to several days to travel to our planet.

Earth has some natural defenses against CMEs. Our magnetic poles tug the magnetized particles toward the north or south. And our atmosphere also prevents most of the particles from reaching the surface. This phenomenon can create beautiful auroras (AKA: the northern lights and southern lights) and are not generally a threat to our planet. However, unusually massive CMEs can wreak havoc.

In the late summer of 1859, the largest solar storms in modern history caused problems on Earth. The Carrington Event! Basically, our planet was bombarded with two huge CMEs. The northern lights, which are usually enjoyed from vantage points in places like Iceland, Greenland, northern Canada, and northern Europe, could be seen in the Caribbean. Magnetic compasses went berserk. The telegraph system in parts of Europe and North America broke down.

The assault of CMEs was more than our magnetic poles could divert. Imagine it this way. If we hold a magnet over three paper clips, all three paper clips will move. If we hold the same magnet over 100 paper clips, not all 100 will be affected.

Perhaps the Carrington Event sounds quite minor to us. We don't rely on telegraphs. We use magnetic compasses only in Scouts or science class and not to navigate the high seas. CMEs don't directly kill humans like volcanoes, diseases, and asteroids potentially can. And who doesn't want to see the northern lights? That sounds cool, not scary. But if we experienced a similar event today, the impact would be more severe. A solar storm this size could knock out power across a continent. Imagine all of North America without electricity. That's not something our local power company could repair in a few hours. It would require weeks or months (possibly years!).

Our reliance on electricity is not just about lights and TV.

The water we drink is sanitized at facilities that need electricity. Hospitals have generators for short-term outages, but a CME event could require a longer recovery. Without a reliable power grid, we cannot access computers and the data they hold. A bank teller cannot look at our account and see if we have any money in savings (and, of course, the ATMs aren't working). A large-scale CME event is all about the apocalyptic aftermath.

The event that occurred in 1859 has been called a 500-year event, meaning it should happen only every 500 years or so. Good news, right? But smaller events occur every fifty years. Luckily, we now have equipment that can hint at possible solar trouble. NASA keeps an eye on the sun for unusual activity, which should give us a few days' notice. A coronal mass ejection takes an average of three days to reach Earth. However, the second CME from the Carrington Event took an express train and reached Earth in seventeen hours. There's also the Deep Space Climate Observatory satellite, which monitors space weather and can warn us fifteen to sixty minutes before a geomagnetic solar storm's arrival. *Plenty of time to avoid a disaster. Maybe.* With warning, satellites can be powered down, electrical grids can be prepared, airplane traffic can be altered, and astronauts can reschedule space walks. (Outside our atmosphere, an astronaut would be in harm's way.)

The sun is responsible for life on Earth, but it also has the power to destroy it. A CME event isn't going to wipe out humans. That's good news. A big one can make life difficult. But eventually, our yellow dwarf will grow up into a star we just can't enjoy. Let's hope our descendants take space travel seriously because *Homo sapiens* will need to be nomadic once again—in about 1 billion years.

CHAPTER 12

OUTER SPACE
SUPERNOVAE, GAMMA-RAY BURSTS, ALIENS

We know the sun will eventually cook our planet, but there's always a chance that something else from the vast universe will destroy humanity first. And since we've already examined asteroids, let's look at other fun extraterrestrial threats.

SUPERNOVAE (THAT'S THE PLURAL OF "SUPERNOVA")

A supernova is simply an exploding star. Though *nova* is misleading because it means "new" in Latin, and these exploding stars are always old. The name is a mistake because centuries ago, people who witnessed these bright blasts of light thought they were *new stars*. Nope, a supernova represents the end. The last hurrah. The final bang. The big send-off.

Supernovae come in two main flavors: Type I (which has three subsets, a, b, and c) and Type II. Not the most creative names, in my opinion. Type Ia involves two stars or a binary star system. Maybe up to half of the Milky Way's solar systems are multi-star (meaning: two or more stars orbiting each other in a fun little dance). A supernova Type Ia occurs when a white dwarf star starts munching on its giant neighboring star's fuel. The white dwarf may be smaller, but it's mighty, with a strong gravitational pull and an appetite for hydrogen and other elements. Eventually, the white dwarf takes too much, and boom! The white dwarf explodes! It's a supernova. Elements and energy are spewed across the universe, and a lucky earthling may observe a sudden bright light in a dark, seemingly empty spot in our sky. It's easier to eye-spy a Type Ia because it can be up to three times more luminous than a Type II.

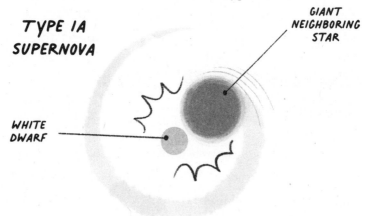

TYPE IA SUPERNOVA

GIANT NEIGHBORING STAR

WHITE DWARF

A Type II supernova is a massive star acting on its own. This star must be at least eight times bigger than our sun to have a chance of going supernova. Little stars need not apply. As these huge stars run out of hydrogen fuel, they go nuclear with other elements. Hydrogen has fused to form helium. Then helium fuses to form carbon. Then we get neon, oxygen, silicon, sulfur, and eventually iron. Once a star begins making iron, it's game over. Depending on the size of the core, the star will explode (go all supernova!) and create a neutron star, which is a twelve-mile-wide star so dense that one teaspoon of it would weigh 50 billion tons. Or, if the star was huge—like twenty-five times bigger than our sun—it will create a black hole. (Confusing side note: Types Ib and Ic do not require a binary system, like Ia. They form because of a core collapse, like a Type II. Their designation as Type I has to do with their lack of hydrogen.)

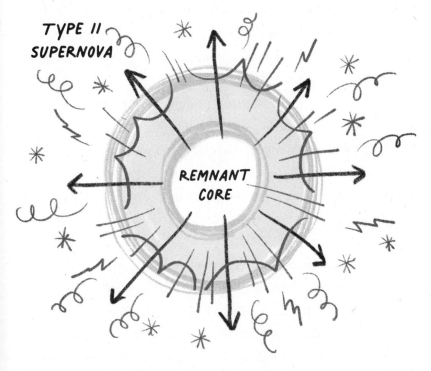

TYPE II
SUPERNOVA

REMNANT
CORE

Our sun is a loner and not part of a binary system, so it can't go supernova Type Ia either. We are not at risk of any kind of supernova in our solar system. But what about neighborhood stars? On average, the Milky Way experiences three supernovae every century. We can't always spot them with our telescopes (even the really big ones) because gas and dust in the center of the galaxy make things blurry. The Milky Way is vast, and luckily none of our closest neighbors are capable of destroying our solar system. *Phew!*

GAMMA-RAY BURSTS

At one time, scientists thought supernovae were the most powerful explosions in the universe. But then they accidentally discovered gamma-ray bursts (GRBs). It was the late 1960s, and the United States launched a satellite to keep tabs on the USSR's nuclear testing. (Remember Chapter 10, when we talked about nuclear bombs and the Cold War.) The satellite looked for gamma rays, and it found some strange waves coming *not* from the other side of the globe but from deep space. These turned out to be gamma-ray bursts. While discovered in the 1960s, GRBs weren't understood for another three decades.

When a supernova occurs, the energy from the explosion travels out in all directions, like the way heat and light radiate from our sun. In a GRB, all that energy is directed into twin beams blasting out in opposite directions. (Imagine a double-bladed lightsaber.) The energy from a ten-second GRB is equivalent to the amount of energy our sun will emit over its 10-billion-year life.

GRBs result from the biggest cosmic catastrophes, like a hypernova, which is a supernova on steroids and ends with the star creating a black hole. These events are possible only in stars that are at least twenty-five times larger than our sun, and they create long GRBs, which last two seconds to a few hours. GRBs can also be created when two neutron stars collide, or a neutron star and a black hole merge to form a bigger black hole. These short GRBs last less than two seconds, so we'd better not blink or we'll miss them. Short bursts are weaker than long bursts and are estimated to happen five times more often.

Back in the 1960s, scientists thought GRBs were rare events. Now NASA satellites catalog about one GRB per day, and astronomers estimate that up to 500 occur daily throughout the universe. Most of these are at the far reaches of the known universe and don't threaten our solar system. But what would happen if a GRB occurred *locally* and had its beam aimed at us? A close GRB, something in our neighborhood of the Milky Way, could be devastatingly lethal.

If directed squarely at Earth, a GRB would destroy a huge portion of our ozone layer and possibly deliver dangerous cosmic rays, which cause radiation sickness—and death—similar to a nuclear explosion. Without our ozone layer, dangerous ultraviolet (UV) rays from the sun would reach Earth's surface—and us. This could result in increased cancers, mutations, and blindness. The UV-B rays entering our world could destroy some small organisms, resulting in a disastrous snowball effect on food chains. And UV-B rays could also alter photosynthesis rates in crops, decreasing food output across the world. Without ozone, most scientists agree, life on Earth would be doomed. But how much depletion can we handle? Hopefully, we'll never find out.

GRBs have yet to be witnessed in the Milky Way. However, it has been suggested that one may have kicked off the Ordovician-Silurian extinction (the first mass extinction) 444 million years ago. The theory is a hypernova explosion within 6,500 light-years of our solar system put Earth in the crosshairs of a GRB, destroying the ozone layer, triggering acid rain, and sparking an ice age. It's a highly debated possibility with no evidence—it's just a theory at this point.

ALIEN INVASION

Beyond Earth, there is no known life in the universe. We have no concrete evidence of plants, animals, or even cells existing anywhere else. But that doesn't mean it's not possible. Our knowledge of space is growing, and the more we learn, the more we realize how much we don't know. Even the map of our galaxy is incomplete, and the Milky Way is one of hundreds of billions of galaxies.

However, since the mid-1990s, astronomers have confirmed the existence of exoplanets (meaning: planets not in our solar system). Most exoplanets revolve around a star or stars, but some are rogue planets (yep, that's what they're called), and they orbit the galactic center instead of a measly star. If there is extraterrestrial life, they'll need an exoplanet to call home. The first confirmed exoplanet to orbit a sun-like star was 51 Pegasi b, and since then, thousands have been verified. But scientists estimate there are millions, maybe billions, or even trillions more. That means there are millions, perhaps billions, or even trillions of potential habitats for life. How exciting!

Our technology doesn't yet allow us to get close enough to these exoplanets to search for evidence of life. But we can still theorize. One scientist turned to mathematics to calculate the possibility of intelligent beings living (or having lived) on another planet in the Milky Way. This is the controversial Drake equation.

$$N = R_* f_p n_e f_l f_i f_c L$$

Let's look at what all these letters (AKA: variables) stand for.

$$N = R_* f_p n_e f_l f_i f_c L$$

N = The answer! The number of possible civilizations in the Milky Way capable of communication. (We're not just looking for life but intelligent life.)

R_* = Rate of star formation. This is how quickly (or slowly) stars are born. Are new ones created every year, every thousand years, every billion years?

f_p = Fraction of stars with planets. Not all stars are parts of solar systems. Some are loners.

n_e = Average number of planets in a solar system that can support life. We're looking for planets in that Goldilocks zone—not so far away from their suns to have only frozen water, not so close all water evaporates. (We're assuming intelligent life doesn't exist without H_2O.)

f_l = Fraction of life-supporting planets that actually sprout life. Just because a planet is in the right zone doesn't mean we'll see life. We need life-making ingredients. Kind of like just because our oven is on doesn't mean we'll have a cake in thirty minutes. We need ingredients.

f_i = Fraction of planets that develop intelligent life. A hospitable planet might have only moss and fungus. We're searching for life with brains.

f_c = Fraction of intelligent civilizations that develop interstellar radio communication. Dolphins and elephants and my dog, Luigi, are smart animals, but they would not be capable of communicating with an alien species through technology.

L = Average length of time a civilization can communicate. Species come and go. So do civilizations. It's possible that a planet *had* intelligent, able-to-communicate life at one time, but not anymore.

Equations are solvable only if we can plug in numbers for the variables. With the Drake equation, scientists are using best guesses, and the answer is not a definite number. No one is saying, "There are exactly 1,789 planets with possible intelligent life." We're looking at the odds that we are not alone.

And you don't need to be a math genius to know that any number multiplied by zero is...ZERO. If we plug a zero into any of the Drake equation variables, we get zero chance of other intelligent life in the universe. That's kind of sad, isn't it?

WHERE AND WHEN

Our current technology allows humans to live on all seven continents of Earth and the International Space Station, which orbits our planet. We have the technology to visit the moon, and there's lots of talk of sending astronauts to Mars in the next few decades. Then that's it. That's the current-ish limit to space exploration involving humans in the pilot seat. We've gone farther with uncrewed vehicles. The NASA spacecraft *Voyager 1* was launched in September 1977, and in 2012, it became the first spacecraft to leave our solar system. And in about 40,000 years, *Voyager 1* will finally approach a star. (It'll pass within 9.3 trillion miles of the star AC+79 3888, but the spacecraft will no longer be operational.)

It's unlikely we will be discovering alien civilizations through space travel. We have a better chance of "hearing" them. Several radio telescopes on Earth are "listening" to deep space for signs of intelligent extraterrestrial life—or at least life that uses radio waves to communicate. Radio waves (which are electromagnetic and not sound waves) travel at the speed of light and continue infinitely through space. They are not generally interrupted by gases or space dust, which mess with visible light waves. Ironically, humans have been sending out radio waves less and less as our technology advances, preferring things like fiber-optic cables. The SETI (Search for Extraterrestrial Intelligence) Institute focuses on a narrow band of radio waves in hopes of eavesdropping on aliens. Still, outer space is vast. Imagine the entire universe is your school, and you are asked to go into the building and find a Pokémon eraser (the eraser represents aliens). So far, you've looked in one desk. That's how much of space we've looked at and listened to. Is there a Pokémon eraser in the school? Is there intelligent life in the universe? Results inconclusive!

Astronomers are looking for aliens, and maybe aliens are looking for us too. Technically, we could be visited by aliens tomorrow, either in-person (or should we say *in-alien?*) or through technology. We can imagine something like a hologram popping up over New York City. It's unlikely but maybe not impossible.

Have you ever considered what our first extraterrestrial visitors may want? Why they've come to Earth? That's a fun dinner conversation! Maybe aliens would want our resources. Maybe they'd want to collect species for their zoo.

Maybe they'd be tourists taking pictures. We won't know what they want until they get here.

Of all the threats coming from space—the death of our sun, asteroids, CMEs, GRBs—alien invasion is at the bottom of my worry list. Honestly, I'm not going to lose sleep over any of these. That's because our most imminent threat is not coming from *out there*. It's coming from within...within our own atmosphere.

In the next section, we will look at our impact on this planet—the only planet in the universe with known life—and consider whether we've sealed our own fate.

PART III

WHAT'S GOING WRONG TODAY

The real and immediate threat to our continued prosperity on Earth is global warming and human-caused climate change. We've seen climate change play a huge role in previous mass extinctions. Dinosaurs and trilobites couldn't prevent (and didn't help create) those devastating events. Humans, however, have thumbs, high-functioning brains, and willpower, which can be used to ignore or fix a problem.

This section will look at the causes of climate change, the potentially catastrophic impact, and the possible solutions. We are running out of time, but for the moment, we still have a choice. We can be the heroes, halting a potential mass extinction. Or we can be the villains of our horror story, ignoring the evidence that's clearly saying, "*Homo sapiens*, you're in trouble!"

CHAPTER 13

GLOBAL WARMING
WHO TURNED UP THE HEAT?

The term "global warming" gets thrown around a lot on the news, in politics, and on social media. Maybe you've heard it in the classroom and at the dinner table too. Yet people often can't define or explain this phenomenon. So let's review the science and terminology. (Definitions? That may sound boring. But stick with me. There's a fart joke ahead.)

WEATHER

This is what's covered on our local news and the info that pops up when we press the cloud icon on a smartphone. Weather pertains to a smallish area and for a shortish term. We want to know if it will rain tomorrow in our town because we have a soccer game. We want to know how much snow to expect (and if school will be canceled for the day).

CLIMATE

Some adults mix up climate and weather, just like they mix up TikTok and Snapchat. Climate is weather during a specific season in a larger region—not only our backyard or town—and over a more extended period, like thirty years. It includes regional temperature, amounts of rain and snow, wind patterns, humidity, and more. And here's the thing: Over this long period, it should be pretty consistent. The climate in Central America is tropical, with a dry season from January through March. The climate in Greenland is arctic, meaning cold and dry. Parts of northern Greenland never get above freezing. Climate does change, but it should happen slooooowly.

The National Oceanic and Atmospheric Administration (NOAA) offers this great and easy way to think about the difference: "Climate is what you expect, weather is what you get."

GLOBAL WARMING

This is simply the rising of Earth's surface temperature. Here, we're looking at the planet as a whole, not at local areas. We know temperatures in Hawaii and Alaska are quite different. This is about the entire Earth, and science has proven that this temperature is warming due to human activity.

CLIMATE CHANGE

This is precisely what the name implies: a change to the climate, including shifts in air temperature, precipitation, wind, ocean currents, and other weather events. When occurring naturally, the change is usually slow over hundreds or thousands of years, like when continents drift toward the poles. But it can happen more quickly too, like when triggered

CELSIUS VS. FAHRENHEIT

In the first two sections of the book, I gave most temperatures in Fahrenheit first (with Celsius often in parenthesis). But in this final section, I'm switching to Celsius because it's what climate scientists (and most of the world) use. I apologize if my inconsistency annoys you. Sorry. *Not sorry.* Um, sorry. We'll get through this together. Here's a handy-dandy conversion chart to guide us.

Common Measurements		
Celsius	Fahrenheit	Notes
–63°	–82°	Average surface temperature of Mars
0°	32°	Water freezes
14°	57°	Average surface temperature of Earth in the twentieth century
35°	95°	Working or playing above this temperature could be deadly
100°	212°	Water boils
464°	867°	Average surface temperature of Venus

Talking Temperature Change		
Celsius	Fahrenheit	Notes
1.0°	1.8°	Earth's temperature rise since the pre-industrial age; climate data from 1850 to 1900 is used for this calculation
1.5°	2.7°	Set in 2018, United Nations' targeted TOTAL maximum temperature rise; includes 1°C we've already experienced
2.0°	3.6°	Set in 2015, Paris Climate Agreement's targeted TOTAL maximum temperature rise; includes 1°C we've already experienced
3.0°–5.0°	5.4°–9.0°	The temperature-rise path we are on if no changes are made to GHG emissions; includes the 1°C we've already experienced

by volcanoes or asteroids. These events—as we know—can lead to mass extinctions. (So maybe we should avoid quick changes. Just a thought.)

The climate change we talk about today is rapid (*uh-oh!*) and driven by humans. A significant portion of the blame comes down to our reliance on fossil fuels.

FOSSIL FUELS

These include crude oil, natural gas, and coal. They're called fossil fuels because they come from fossilized material, such as dead animals and plants. These long-dead organisms have been buried for millions of years under high pressure, and now they're ready to be turned into energy for our homes, schools, factories, and vehicles. But when we burn this coal or gas or oil, carbon (and other stuff) is released into our atmosphere at unnatural rates. (Remember our often-repeated rule from Chapter 2 about what happens when CO_2 increases?)

ATMOSPHERE

Our planet is wrapped in a protective layer composed of nitrogen (78 percent), oxygen (21 percent), and a handful of other essential gases. We already talked about how our atmosphere protects us from smallish asteroids and solar radiation. (Thank you, atmosphere!) It also maintains our just-right temperature, letting in enough heat and light from the sun to keep us warm and allowing some heat and light to escape back into space. Without this protective layer, the planet would be frozen and probably lifeless, like Mars. (Thank you *again*, atmosphere!) The right balance of gases in the atmosphere is crucial for a healthy planet. Unfortunately, humans are altering the atmosphere's chemical composition by emitting greenhouse gases (GHGs), like CO_2, into the air.

GREENHOUSE GASES

If you've ever sat in a closed-up car in the bright sunshine, you've experienced a greenhouse effect. The windows allow light and heat from the sun into the vehicle, then the light and heat become trapped inside, causing you to get sweaty and probably stinky. In the summer, car temperatures can be hot enough to kill. Never leave a pet (or a human) in a closed-up vehicle in warm weather.

Earth's atmosphere also works like a greenhouse—*again*, this is a good thing because we don't want to be like Mars. But we also don't want to be like Venus. (Venus's heavy atmosphere is mostly CO_2, and the average temperature is 464°C.) Too many greenhouse gases in our atmosphere will make Earth like a car on a hot, sunny day. More heat will be trapped and less will escape into space.

EXOSPHERE

THERMOSPHERE

MESOSPHERE

STRATOSPHERE

OZONE LAYER

TROPOSPHERE

Our most common GHGs are

- **carbon dioxide** (human sources: burning fossil fuels, wood, and other materials)
- **methane** (human sources: burning coal, decaying trash, and raising livestock—includes cow burps)
- **nitrous oxide** (human sources: running power plants and making fertilizers)
- **fluorinated gas** (human sources: refrigeration, air-conditioning, and manufacturing—f-gases are not found in nature)
- **water vapor** (human sources; none directly, but warmer air holds more water vapor, and humans have made the Earth warmer—it's called a feedback process)

The more of these gases we have in our atmosphere, the worse the greenhouse effect. To put it simply, we need to cut GHG emissions.

EMISSIONS

This reminds me of an old joke. A man is at the doctor's office.

DOCTOR:

What's the problem?

MAN:

I suffer from silent gas emissions, and it's getting worse.

DOCTOR:

How so?

MAN:

Last week, I had about a dozen silent gas emissions every day.

DOCTOR:

Oh.

MAN:

Then yesterday, I had about thirty, including ten silent gas emissions during dinner.

DOCTOR:

My word.

MAN:

And since talking to you, I've had three silent gas emissions.

DOCTOR:

Wow.

MAN:

So what do you think, Doc?

DOCTOR:

First things first. We're getting your hearing tested.

Haha. Fart joke. But gas emissions—the non-flatulence kind—are a major problem for our planet. These human activities are the biggest contributors to GHG emissions.

- Energy used by industry   24.2%
Basically, this is everything humans manufacture in factories: cars, iPhones, bread (but not growing the wheat), paper, steel, and machines for other factories.

- Agriculture and land use   18.4%
This broad category covers much of what humans do outside: raising livestock, growing crops (the food kind and non-food kind, like cotton), destroying forests and wetlands, and crop burning.

- Electricity and heat for buildings   17.5%
This is the electricity we use at home, school, offices, shops, basketball arenas, and so on. It's for heating, cooking, lights, computers, and everything else that turns on.

- Transportation   16.2%
This includes human travel and freight travel by road, rail, air, and sea.

Note: These numbers can be shuffled and reorganized. For example, food production can be considered responsible for 25 percent of GHG emissions when we combine the agriculture part (example: raising chickens), the industry portion (turning chickens into nuggets), the transportation portion (getting the chickens from the farm to the factory and then getting the nuggets to the store and to your house), and the electricity and heat portion (cooking your nuggets).

Some reports have estimated that cooling (which falls under the heat category—ironic, I know) is responsible for 10 percent of emissions. Think about that awful loop. We're making our planet warmer, and to combat the heat, we're running more air conditioners and fans, which leads to more emissions, which leads to warmer temperatures, which leads to…you get it.

These silent gas emissions are destroying our planet. We need to stop farting around and get them in check.

CO_2 EMISSIONS

In 2019, the world broke a record. The atmospheric carbon dioxide hit 409 parts per million. That's the highest it's been in 3 million years. And we did that. Humans!

But this is not a record we want to break (or to continue to break). In the mid-eighteenth century, before the industrial revolution, atmospheric CO_2 was approximately 280 parts per million. And since then, the planet's temperature has gone up 1°C. Now, we may be tempted to say, "Eh, one degree is nothing. You can't even feel that." But think about it this way: At 0°C, water will freeze all day long. At 1°C, *fugetaboutit*. We just have really cold water. One degree matters!

If we want to get global warming in check, we need to get carbon emissions in check (as well as those other GHGs). The Union of Concerned Scientists wants us, as a planet, to achieve net-zero carbon emissions by 2050. That means whatever we pump into the air, we also suck back out. Before we suggest covering all of North America in trees, we still need to cut our emissions. If our house were flooding, we wouldn't just grab more buckets; we'd need to repair the leak.

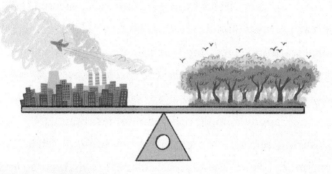

NOT ALL EQUAL

GHG emissions vary across the world. The top polluting countries are, in order of mostest to leastest, China, the USA, the European Union (twenty-seven countries in Europe), India, Russia, Japan, Brazil, Indonesia, Iran, and Canada. This group emits two-thirds of the world's GHGs and is only about half the world's population. Of course, global warming and the problem of climate change are not isolated to the regions where gases originate. Like if someone pees in the pool, the problem affects every swimmer. (Diarrhea would be a better analogy, if you want to be really gross about it.)

And even if we stopped pumping greenhouse gases into the atmosphere today, Earth's temperature would still rise for decades. A lot of carbon dioxide is already in our air and oceans, and it's going to take some time to rebalance the planet.

CLIMATE GOALS TAKE TEAMWORK

In 2015, representatives from 196 countries gathered in Paris for a conference about our climate crisis. They agreed that global warming is real and that climate change is bad for our species. *(Science! Bringing thinking people together for millennia!)* They determined global warming should be held below a 2°C rise, and we should really aim for less than 1.5°C. That's measuring temperature change from pre-industrial times. Remember, we've already passed the 1°C marker, so we're not starting at zero. And if we take the no-change-to-gas-emissions path, we are heading for a 3°C to 5°C temperature bump by the end of the century.

To achieve the 2°C goal, countries agreed to cut their emissions, and each nation set its own target. The US aimed to cut GHG output to 26 to 28 percent of what it was in 2005—and to do this by 2025. However, even though most countries signed the agreement (as of 2021, only two sovereign nations have not signed: Syria and Nicaragua), there was no punishment for not achieving these individual goals. No reward either, unless we consider a habitable planet a reward in itself.

This is like a giant group project where everyone is expected to do their part, but no one gets in trouble with the teacher if they don't. We all know how that usually goes.

A few countries took their goals and responsibilities seriously. According to Climate Action Tracker, Morocco and The Gambia are making strides to meet the more challenging 1.5°C target. But they were not major contributors of GHGs even before the conference. To have any chance of keeping global warming to less than 2°C, the planet needed the big players—*we're looking at you, China and the USA!*—to step up and crush their emissions goals. But that's not what happened. Instead, in 2017, the president of the United States infamously declared that the country would be leaving the Paris Agreement as soon as possible—which, for legal reasons, was set for November 4, 2020. (The US would rejoin in 2021 under a new president, and set even more ambitious goals for reducing greenhouse gas emissions.)

Then in 2018, a mere three years after the Paris conference and during America's we're-not-playing-along phase, the United Nations came out with a new report that said 2°C of warming would stink. It would mean disaster for much of the planet and the *Homo sapiens* who live there. The UN adjusted its aim and said that 1.5°C of warming has to be the new target if we want a healthy Earth.

I wish I could say: *After this report, countries regrouped and created better plans. Nations made cross-my-heart-and-hope-to-die promises to reduce greenhouse gas emissions. They listened to the science and took immediate action. No more waiting because they knew time was running out. Like in some great alien invasion movie, all citizens of Earth came together as one and fought to save the place we call home.*

Of course, none of this happened (not the alien invasion or the immediate action on climate change). Humanity is still waiting for its moment to rise up and fight the problem it created.

USA BY THE NUMBERS

The Paris Climate Agreement allows each country to set its own targets for GHG emissions. Here's where the United States stands.

GHG Emissions Reduction from 2005 Levels

Initial Goal Set in 2015	26–28% by 2025
New Goal Set in 2021	50–52% by 2030
Current Progress (as of 2019)	13%

CONTROVERSY

Scientists are overwhelmingly in agreement on global warming: Humans are to blame! Ninety-seven percent of climate scientists say global warming and accompanying climate change are driven by our activities. To put it even more bluntly, here's what Dr. Kate Marvel of NASA's Goddard Institute for Space Studies said: "We are more sure that greenhouse gas is causing climate change than we are that smoking causes cancer." (And smoking definitely causes cancer!)

When regular, nonexpert folks are surveyed about human-caused climate change, we don't find the same overwhelming agreement. The percentage of believers varies by education and political party. Perhaps some people struggle to accept climate change because they've personally experienced an unusually cold summer. (Of course, we know that this is *weather*, not climate.) Or perhaps some people have read articles or watched videos about natural warm spells and ice ages in Earth's past, which have happened. This is true. Earth's climate fluctuates over loooooong periods of time. But the climate change science is also true.

- Earth's temperature is rising faster now than it has in the past 2,000 years.
- Carbon dioxide levels are higher now than at any time in the last 3 million years.

- Humans have been pumping CO_2 and other GHGs into the air since the dawn of the industrial age.
- Even after the ratification of the Paris Climate Agreement, global CO_2 emissions increased between 2015 and 2018.

We know better, and yet we're still doing it.

WEATHER AND CLIMATE— AN ANALOGY

We know weather and climate aren't the same thing, and this analogy from the *New York Times* is an excellent way to illustrate the difference.

Weather is immediate. Here! Now! It's like the money we have in our pocket. We can spend it right here, right now.

Climate is broader and something for the long run. It's like the money we have in the bank. We keep it there for a while.

Occasionally, we may experience an unusual, freezing-cold day. (The definition of "unusual, freezing-cold day" really depends on our location. An unusual, freezing-cold day in Florida is different from an unusual, freezing-cold day in Wyoming.) This doesn't mean global warming isn't real or that it's over, unfortunately. A cold day—or even a handful of cold days—is just weather. It's a short-term situation (weather) and not an explanation of the big picture (climate).

Now, let's imagine we have a million dollars in our savings account, but one day, we go out shopping and forget our wallet. This doesn't mean we're totally broke. We just don't have any cash *right now*, and we won't be buying any comic books or Kit Kats on this outing. It's a short-term situation (pocket money) and not an explanation of the big picture (bank savings).

CHAPTER 14

1.5°C TO 2°C
JUST A WEE BIT WARMER

IT'S GOOD TO HAVE GOALS

We know the Paris Climate Agreement goal: to keep global warming to an increase of *less than* 2°C from pre-industrial levels. (And again, we should really not exceed 1.5°C.) Unfortunately, no one thinks we can do this. We're already 1°C warmer. If we continue our current CO_2 output levels, a 5°C bump by the end of the century is likely. A 6°C rise (or higher) is not out of the question. So what will a warmer Earth look like?

WILD, WACKY WEATHER

Extreme weather will be the first real taste of climate change for most of us, and it's already happening in places across the globe. Don't worry if you haven't noticed yet, because it's gonna get worse soon.

TORRENTIAL RAINS AND FLOODING!

We all deal with rainy days and don't give much thought to them unless it's going to mess with our lacrosse schedule. But thanks to climate change, our warm air can hold more moisture, so when it rains, it has the potential to pour. More precipitation can lead to increased flooding near coasts and rivers and in urban areas. (All that pavement cannot absorb H_2O the way a grassy field might.) FYI, most cars can be swept away in as little as twelve inches of water.

HURRICANES!

These storms love warm ocean water. As Earth heats up, scientists don't expect *more* hurricanes (*yay!*), but they do predict more intense hurricanes (*boo!*). Hurricanes are judged on a one-to-five scale, with five being the *worst*, and in the future, fours and fives are going to be more common. A

Category 4 is capable of ripping roofs off buildings. A Category 5 has winds over 157 miles per hour and can bulldoze houses.

SNOWSTORMS!

The planet is getting warmer, yet extreme snowstorms are still a thing—and a more *frequent* thing in the northeastern United States. The reason, again, is that warmer air holds more water, even in winter. When cold arctic air slowly moves south and becomes friendly with moisture-rich warm air coming off the ocean, massive snowstorms form. The media loves to give these storms hashtag-worthy names like Snowmageddon, Snowpocalypse, and Snowzilla. Perhaps in the future, we'll see Snowtastrophe and Snowkenstein. (Okay, that last one doesn't really work.)

~~Fun~~ Frightening Facts:

- Flooding has killed over 950 Americans in the past decade.

- In 2017, Hurricane Harvey dumped 15 percent more rain on Houston than it would have in a pre–global warming world.

- From 2008 to 2018, the northeastern United States experienced twenty-seven major snowstorms. That's over three times more than in previous decades.

- Interestingly, scientists have not found clear evidence of increased tornado activity or severity due to climate change. (This area of extreme weather needs more research and data—tornado tracking is kind of new.)

FIRE!

Science 101 *and* Camping 101: Dry stuff burns better than wet stuff. A 2°C warming means increased droughts worldwide, which means drier plants, *which* means lots of potential kindling for fires. A lightning strike can ignite a blaze, or careless humans can do the damage. In 2017, a man in Arizona started a wildfire by shooting his rifle at an explosive target as part of a gender-reveal party. The resulting fire burned 47,000 acres, cost over $8 million in damages, and got the guy in a lot of trouble. And in 2020, a gender-reveal event used a pyrotechnic device that started the El Dorado Fire (AKA: the Gender-Reveal Fire). That blaze burned over 20,000 acres, destroyed five homes, and killed one firefighter.

Wildfires also create a vicious cycle. As trees burn, they release carbon into the air. And, of course, every tree that is destroyed means we have one less carbon-sucking organism. It's like a double whammy.

~~Fun~~ Frightening Facts:

- Wildfires in the United States are burning twice as much area annually as fires did between 1985 and 1999.
- The US fire season is seventy-eight days longer than it was fifty years ago.
- Between 1992 and 2015, lightning strikes caused 44 percent of the wildfires in the western US.
- Humans and our mistakes cause most of the wildfires in the US. However, lightning-triggered fires cause more damage.

NASTY SURPRISES

Have you ever had anthrax? The disease causes fever, chills, sore throat, headache, fatigue, vomiting (perhaps bloody vomiting), and diarrhea (perhaps bloody diarrhea). It ain't pretty...and you've probably never had it. Anthrax is almost unheard of in North America and Europe. But in 2016, a twelve-year-old boy in the Yamal Peninsula in Russia died of anthrax, and about 100 others were hospitalized. Here's what scientists believe happened. Seventy-five years earlier, a reindeer with anthrax croaked. The Yamal Peninsula is above the Arctic Circle, so the animal carcass froze and remained frozen

until climate change brought a heat wave to the region. The reindeer's body thawed, and while the reindeer did not come back to life (no one likes a zombie reindeer), the anthrax bacteria woke up. The disease contaminated water and soil, which infected over 2,000 modern-day reindeer, and then it spread to humans.

Anthrax is not the only potential frozen threat awaiting a warm day. RNA fragments of the Spanish flu have been discovered in mass graves in Alaska. The permafrost in Siberia might be an icy hibernation spot for smallpox and bubonic plague. As we know from Chapter 8, we have a vaccine for smallpox, but it is no longer distributed because the disease was eradicated decades ago. And then there are bacteria and viruses trapped in ice that humans don't know about yet. Things we've never seen! Thanks to climate change, we may have to share our planet with deadly, new-to-us microscopic threats.

~~Fun~~ Frightening Facts:

- Scientists have found 30,000-year-old viruses in Siberian permafrost. Luckily, these still-contagious buggers only like to infect amoebas (meaning: a type of single-celled organism).

- Scientists have revived an 8-million-year-old bacterium that was discovered dormant on a glacier. (Thankfully, this was done in a secure lab.)

- Since the start of the twenty-first century, temperatures in the Arctic have risen twice as fast as the rest of the planet.

SICK SEAS

Our world is 71 percent water, and our oceans are taking the brunt of our human-caused climate change. Scientists estimate that the oceans absorb 90 percent of the planet's warming. (Thank you, oceans!) They're also sucking up extra CO_2—as much as 30 percent of what we pump into the air—and becoming more acidic. (Thank you again, oceans! Or maybe we should say, "Sorry, oceans.") This is bad news for any critter with a shell or protective skeleton. (And don't get me started on the islands of plastics polluting our water.) At just 1.5°C of warming, we will lose 70 to 90 percent of our tropical coral reefs. Our oceans are sick! That's 71 percent of our planet that's not feeling so good.

~~Fun~~ Frightening Facts:

- Over half a billion people rely on coral reefs for food, income, or natural protection from weather events.
- About 25 percent of fish species spend at least part of their life cycle in coral reef ecosystems.
- Like on land, the oceans can have heat waves, and our planet is experiencing a 54 percent increase in watery heat-wave days compared to a century ago.

RISING TIDES

Rising tides are a favorite topic whenever scientists are interviewed about the impact of climate change. Our oceans are rising for two reasons. First, warm water takes up more room than cold water.

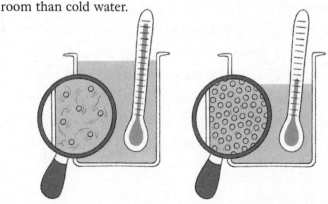

Second, as ice sheets melt, the resulting water is added to our oceans. Let's imagine the unthinkable: All of Earth's ice melts. Ocean levels could rise over 216 feet! Coastal cities like New York, Venice, Tokyo, and Mumbai would be flooded and portions unlivable. Florida would be totally under water. But even with current warming trends, this is a worst-case scenario and not something that can happen overnight. It would take 5,000 years. Does that mean we should leave the nightmare to our great-great-great-great-grandchildren? If we do, I think they'll be disappointed in us.

Unfortunately, we're already stuck in a rising-ocean cycle. The carbon in the air and the upward temperature trends cannot easily be corrected. It's not like flipping a light switch. Imagine we're boiling a pot of water on the stove, and then we turn off the burner. The water is not instantly room temperature. (Definitely don't stick your finger in that water when the bubbles are gone just to prove our point.) Earth is similar but more complicated. If we stopped dumping carbon and other greenhouse gases into the air today, we would still have to live with the damage we've already done.

Depending on what actions humans take now, ocean levels might rise less than a foot by 2100—still a problem but a more manageable problem—or we might require a ladder to take measurements. Rising seas and storms will batter coastal cities, but they will fare better than some islands. In the next century, the Maldives and the Marshall Islands could be washed away.

~~Fun~~ Frightening Facts:

- Since 1880, global sea levels have risen by eight to nine inches.
- Worst-case scenario (and keeping with current GHG emissions), seas could rise 8.2 feet above their year 2000 levels by the end of the century.
- By 2050, over 150 million people will live in an area lower than the high-tide line, making them targets for devastating floods.
- Of the ten largest cities on the planet, eight are considered coastal.

DEADLY HEAT WAVES

Humans can function (and survive!) only at specific temperatures. Our upper limit is about 35°C (95°F) in high humidity. And at this temperature, all we can tolerate is sitting still and guzzling water. Humans should not work or play when it's this hot. To keep cool, your body sweats and your blood rushes to the skin. With your blood diverting from its usual course, you may feel dizzy, have a headache, or want to throw up. If you don't cool down, your internal organs will turn off to save energy. This includes your brain. You won't be thinking very clearly. (Have you ever been in a classroom on a hot day? It's hard to concentrate!) And things can get really bad from here. With severe heatstroke, vital organs can swell and suffer permanent damage, and without treatment, it can lead to death.

~~Fun~~ Frightening Facts:

- Earth is warming faster now than it has in millions of years.
- Currently in the US, heat waves kill more people than any other extreme weather. Approximately 12,000 Americans die prematurely each year from heat-related causes.
- Deadly heat waves affect 30 percent of the world's population today, and by 2100, this figure could grow to 75 percent.
- The hottest temperature ever recorded on Earth was in August 2020, at Furnace Creek in Death Valley, California; it reached 54°C (130°F).

ANIMAL EXTINCTION

Climate change is making it harder to share this planet with animals, especially the large ones. Bigger animals need bigger habitats. Sometimes we knowingly reduce their habitats through deforestation and development (like making farms, building housing, and putting in shopping centers). Sometimes we do it "accidentally" through climate change. Plants and animals are going extinct at a faster rate now than at any time in the past 10 million years. Large animals do not adapt quickly, and all these changes are happening too fast for them to adjust.

A few of our favorite big animal buddies (like those in stories and movies) are particularly at risk.

AFRICAN ELEPHANTS (LIKE DUMBO!)

African elephants need thirty to fifty gallons of water per day for drinking, plus more for playing, bathing, and cooling off. Rising temperatures in the savannas are causing droughts and water shortages. Elephants, like humans, cannot survive long without H_2O.

GIANT PANDAS (LIKE PO!)

Giant pandas will likely be forced to move north as temperatures rise and make conditions unlivable on their current turf in China. However, giant pandas eat mostly bamboo. Plants, which lack feet, cannot migrate as quickly as animals. As pandas move, there might not be enough for them to eat in their new locations.

POLAR BEARS (LIKE THE COCA-COLA BEARS!)

Polar bears cannot outswim a ringed seal—their favorite meal. They hunt by waiting on the sea ice for a seal to emerge for a breath, and then they can attack. Melting ice in the Arctic will mean starvation for Earth's largest land carnivore.

TIGERS (LIKE TIGGER!)

Tigers are already an endangered species due to loss of habitat, hunting, and other human meddling. Less than 4,000 remain in the wild today; their numbers were over 100,000 a century ago. For the Sundarbans tigers on the Indian and

Bangladeshi coasts, climate change is a direct and imminent threat to their habitat. The locally predicted one-foot rise in sea level by the year 2070 will completely wash away their territory, leaving them homeless.

~~Fun~~ Frightening Facts:

- At a 2°C temperature rise, 5 percent of Earth's species are threatened with extinction.

- Humans have altered 75 percent of the land on Earth.

- Since 1500, at least 680 vertebrate species (animals with backbones) have gone extinct—that we know of.

- Only 3 percent of vertebrate life on Earth is wild. The other 97 percent are humans, pets, and farm animals (mostly farm animals).

BREAK OUT THE BUG SPRAY

Mosquitoes and ticks are two creatures that love the idea of a warmer world. Put it this way: Winter is not their favorite season. And these pests carry and spread disease. Species of mosquitoes are responsible for yellow fever, West Nile virus, Zika, and malaria. These mosquitoes (and the diseases they carry) mainly stick to the hot spots near the equator and tropics. But as the temperature warms, these bugs will have expanding habitats and new humans to infect. By 2050, half the world's population will be in their bite zone.

Lyme disease is spread by ticks and has been a problem in the northeastern US for decades. This disease can be mild, with itching and pain, or it can be severe, with brain inflammation and heart palpitations. Some victims experience lifelong complications. As Earth has warmed and northern winters have become milder, the ticks and their diseases have multiplied and spread geographically.

~~Fun~~ Frightening Facts:

- The mosquito is the world's deadliest animal.
- *Aedes aegypti*, a mosquito species responsible for yellow fever and Zika, can be found in warm states like Florida, Texas, California, and Arizona. Because of warming temperatures, it will likely be found in Chicago by midcentury.
- About 300,000 Americans are diagnosed annually with Lyme disease.

A-PACKING WE WILL GO

With coastal regions flooded, some cities too hot to handle, and other areas ravaged by extreme weather, humans will be forced to migrate. And while we're pretty mobile animals with our two legs and rolling suitcases, politics does not make it easy. Crossing international borders requires paperwork and money, and scientists predict that those most affected by climate change will be the people with the lowest incomes. Some studies suggest that there will be an increase in conflict and war as humans try to find livable places to relocate. Talk about making a bad situation worse. Imagine if all the people of North America and South America needed to find new homes in the upper United States or

Canada. Would everyone be welcomed? Would Americans and Canadians be willing to share resources and land?

~~Fun~~ Frightening Facts:

- By 2050, 143 million people from three areas of the world will become climate migrants: 86 million from sub-Saharan Africa, 40 million from South Asia, and 17 million from Latin America.
- By 2100, 13 million Americans could be forced to relocate because of rising sea levels. Miami and New Orleans are likely to take the worst hit. .

1.5°C VS. 2°C

The Paris Climate Agreement set the global temperature rise limit to 2°C or less. But shortly after, a scientific report urged the world to keep it below 1.5°C. A half a degree Celsius doesn't sound significant, but this is what it would mean for our planet.

	At 1.5°C (2.7°F)	At 2°C (3.6°F)
Sea Ice	1 in 100 summers without sea ice	1 in 10 summers without sea ice
Extreme Heat	14% of the world's population will be exposed to severe heat every five years	37% of the world's population will be exposed to severe heat every five years
Plants	8% of plants will lose half their habitable land	16% of plants will lose half their habitable land
Vertebrates	4% of vertebrates will lose half their habitable land	8% of vertebrates will lose half their habitable land
Insects	6% of insects will lose half their habitable land	18% of insects will lose half their habitable land
Coral Reefs	70–90% will be destroyed	99% will be destroyed

TOTALLY TERRIFYING

All the information in this chapter is meant to be terrifying. It's scary because it's true! Fear is a good motivator. It's what makes you run away from a bear and hand in your homework on time. (But sadly, you cannot outrun a bear...or your teacher.) If enough of us fear for our future and our planet's future, maybe we can alter our self-made destructive path. Perhaps we can clean up this mess. But we've got some work to do.

~~Fun~~ Frightening Facts:

- Globally, 2020 and 2016 (basically) tied for the hottest year on record.

- Globally, the 2010s were the hottest decade on record.

- Globally, the 2020s will be the decade *Homo sapiens* get their act together. (A little wishful thinking.)

CHAPTER 15

WE'RE DOOMED
(JK, HOW TO SAVE THE ~~PLANET~~ PEOPLE)

We're not doomed...yet! Here's the thing. This whole life-on-Earth experiment is a single trial run. Typically when we do a science experiment, it's advisable to repeat the process to prove the results. But we can't do that because we have only one Earth and one species of humans. We are living this experiment.

In this final chapter, we're going to explore how we can save our species and our planet. (Well, Earth is not in jeopardy of disappearing because of humans. We can't give ourselves that much credit. But we can certainly make it uninhabitable for ourselves and other critters. Earth is here to stay—until, maybe, the sun goes red giant. See Chapter 11.) We need to adjust our behavior before nature sends us into a terrifying time-out.

CARBON FOOTPRINT

When we walk across sand, we leave footprints behind. As we live our CO_2-loving lives, we leave a carbon footprint behind. This is our individual (or household) contribution to global warming. (It should be noted that carbon footprint is not just about carbon or carbon dioxide but all greenhouse gases.) In general, an average American contributes 14.8 tons of GHGs annually to the environment. The world average is 4.9 tons per person. Humans need to collectively reduce greenhouse gas emissions by at least 7 percent each year throughout the 2020s.

Want to know your carbon footprint? The internet is filled with carbon footprint calculators to help us determine our own impact. Most of these calculators are complicated and require information that you'd have to dig around for, like your annual electric bill and what type of power plant supplies your electricity. Sounds like a fun Friday-night family project to me.

In the meantime, here are some ways to clean up your carbon footprint.

PLAY WITH THE THERMOSTAT

By one estimate, residential buildings contribute about 11 percent of greenhouse gas emissions. This is the electricity and heat used in our homes. There are plenty of little ways to reduce our carbon footprint here, like doing homework in the dark and taking cold, short showers. In seriousness, keeping a house less toasty in the winter (set the thermostat lower) and more balmy in the summer (set the thermostat higher) can cut heating and cooling bills and lower our carbon footprint slightly.

EVIL PLASTIC!

If we pause from reading for a second and look around, we can probably see dozens of plastic items in our immediate area.

I'm typing on a plastic keyboard. On my desk, I have plastic eyeglasses, a tape dispenser, a cell phone case, a Magic 8 Ball (for when I have to make hard decisions), pens, and Legos (a mini telescope with a figurine of the scientist Nancy Grace Roman). Plastics are everywhere, cheap, and useful. (IMHO, glass Legos would never work.) Plastics are also littering our planet on both land and sea and contributing to global warming. In 2019, the GHG emissions from the making and destroying of plastics was equal to 189 coal-powered plants. It's estimated that plastic use will go up in the next three decades. We can do our part by selecting reusable items. Let's limit (or even eliminate!) our single-use plastics, like straws, forks, grocery bags, bottles, food containers, sandwich wrap, and goody-bag toys. A plastic item should have a purpose that lasts longer than the average movie preview.

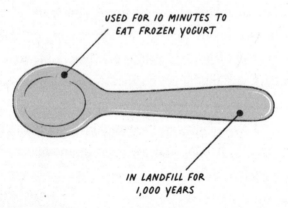

USED FOR 10 MINUTES TO EAT FROZEN YOGURT

IN LANDFILL FOR 1,000 YEARS

A ONE-WAY TICKET!

Transportation accounts for about 16 percent of emissions, and this category is trending up. One solution is to stay home and spend our days connecting with others on the internet. Oh, wait, we did this in 2020; not to combat global warming, of course, but to control the COVID-19 pandemic. In April 2020, when many locations mandated a lockdown and people hung out on their couches all day, global greenhouse emissions fell somewhere between 10 and 30 percent. For the year, global CO_2 emissions were 6.4 percent less than in 2019, and in the United States, they dropped 13 percent because Americans curbed their driving habits. Unfortunately, a month isn't long enough to see a lasting difference, and even a 6.4 percent decrease misses our global goal of 7 percent. (Plus, emissions rebounded in 2021.) Still, we can make small changes in our own behavior, like walking instead of driving, taking a bike instead of a plane, and sailing on a paddle boat instead of a yacht.

All joking aside, little efforts do help. Next time we're in the car waiting to pick up a sibling, we can cut the engine. And if we fly (one of the worst activities for the environment), we can purchase a carbon-emission offset to balance our environmental impact. Here's how it works. A flight from New York to London dumps about .33 metric tons of CO_2 into the atmosphere per passenger, so we donate to an organization that will "remove" .33 metric tons of CO_2 from the atmosphere. However, the organization doesn't technically remove the gases. It invests in programs that will save forests, plant trees, bring clean energy into villages, reduce methane from landfills, and so on, thus offsetting the environmental impact of our flight.

CHEW ON THIS!

What we eat affects emissions and global warming. Let's talk about cows—or, as a butcher would call them, beef. The world has about 1 billion cattle and that number's growing. All those cows burp and fart methane gas—more so in burps than in farts. Grazing animals contribute 40 percent of the anthropogenic (meaning: influenced by humans) methane spit into the atmosphere. But it's not just stinky burps that put greenhouse gases in the air. There are also emissions from producing meat (going from calf to cow to hamburgers) and then getting that food to stores. Each time we eat a serving of beef, we're dumping an estimated 6.61 pounds of greenhouse gases into the air. Compare that to eggs, which generate .89 pounds of gases, rice at .16 pounds, and carrots at .07 pounds. If we eat less beef and other animal products, we can cut our individual carbon footprint. Some families, and even some schools, celebrate Meatless Monday. Being a part-time vegetarian is a good start to helping the environment.

THE BIG STUFF

To significantly slow global warming, there must be large, coordinated efforts by countries across the planet. We need teamwork, like the kind started by the Paris Climate Agreement. We can reduce our personal impact, and that matters, but not everyone is aware of their contributions to the problem, and some people are just set in their ways. Real changes need to be governed and enforced. (I mean, let's be honest. I'd probably speed if there weren't speed limits. I like to go fast, and I'm often running late.)

OH, THE POLITICS OF CLIMATE CHANGE

Unfortunately, even though the scientific community is in agreement over the cause of global warming, it's become a political issue. It seems that certain world leaders don't see (or believe in) the value of a healthy Earth that can sustain human life in the long run—not if it requires any economic sacrifices. Some developing countries view it as unfair to have environmental restrictions on their citizens and businesses as they're just starting out economically, when Great Britain, the United States, and other first-world countries did not have environmental restrictions during their transitions into industrial nations.

On a more local level, elected officials may prioritize immediate problems over long-term climate issues. If people are hungry or out of work right now, government leaders need to address those problems first. However, we cannot continue to sacrifice our future in favor of easier solutions today. The choice should not be success today *or* success tomorrow. It can be both. Green energy can create new jobs. Transportation can be efficient and environmentally friendly. Raising crops for humans to consume instead of for cows to consume can feed more people.

CLEAN ENERGY

Let's imagine for a minute that all the people in all the land decide climate change needs immediate action, and we're willing to invest in our species' future. Our first focus should be on clean energy. The electricity running into our homes needs to come from non-greenhouse-gas-making power plants. There are options like solar, wind, hydro, and nuclear. None are perfect (or cheap), but we'll find better solutions if we move in the green direction. Technology will improve. Scientific knowledge will expand.

It's not just the electricity powering our homes and schools that needs to change. Manufacturing must also draw its energy from clean sources. And waste created during industrial processes should be limited—or better yet, eliminated.

We will never return to a nomadic society where we all walk around on our own two feet or use animals. So we need to improve our transportation—not making cars go faster but making all vehicles less pollute-y. Trucks, trains, boats, and planes will have to meet stricter standards for emissions.

Then there's the agriculture issue. We've talked about this a lot already. Humans need to change the way we eat and the way we grow our food. Through technology and smart decision making, we can free up land from agriculture and return it to a *natural* state and still feed our booming population.

SOME WACKY IDEAS TO SLOW CLIMATE CHANGE

BLOCK OUT THE SUN

In the summer, people place windshield screens in their cars to block out the sun and keep the interiors cooler. (While the cars are parked, not while driving, of course.) Could we do this for Earth? It has been suggested that we could fill our atmosphere with particles to block out the sun. We'd make every day a cloudy day. In the past, this happened naturally after some notable volcanic eruptions, including those that caused mass extinctions. But what could we put in the air to create an eternally cloudy day that would not make people and animals sick? What are we willing to breathe in? Currently, there are no safe answers, but the National Academies of Sciences, Engineering, and Medicine recommend that the US government spend $100 million researching solar geoengineering.

SEAWEED

As we know, cows burp (and fart, to a lesser extent) methane, which is an environmental issue. Methane is eighty-six times more efficient at warming the atmosphere than CO_2. When bovines chew and digest grasses, the reaction happens naturally. Scientists have come up with a wild solution of adding red seaweed to cows' feed. Cows still burp, but the result is less methane. Up to 95 percent less methane. Simple solution, right? We'll just need to move all the cows to the sea or start growing seaweed in fields in Iowa.

CARBON CAPTURE

If only there was a way to capture CO_2 from the air and dispose of it somewhere else. Well, good news, this technology exists. Bad news, it's expensive, experimental, and not available on a grand scale. One plant in Iceland uses giant fans to collect carbon dioxide from the air. Then the CO_2 is mixed with water and pumped deep into the basalt rock underground. Basalt is porous (meaning: it has a lot of holes), and it's created when lava cools. Two years after the holey basalt is filled with the carbon-water solution, it becomes solid rock. Once the Icelandic plant is fully operational, it will pull 4,000 tons of CO_2 from the air and turn it into rock. That's a great start. However, in 2020, the US emitted 4.5 billion metric tons of CO_2—and 2020 was a light year due to COVID.

That means we would need over a million carbon capture plants like the one in Iceland to suck out America's annual portion of CO_2 emissions.

A more established technology is carbon capture storage. It doesn't use fans to scrub the air but instead involves snagging CO_2 directly from fossil-fuel power plants before it's released into the atmosphere. This process can capture over 90 percent of the CO_2 waste. But the carbon dioxide can't be put in giant balloons and sent into space. It first must be turned into a liquid, and then it can be transported through pipelines or on trucks. But to where? The final step is finding a place to throw it out. One option is to put it deep into the Earth's crust, perhaps in voids where humans have already removed gas, oil, or coal. Problem solved? Not quite.

There's a cost to carbon capture storage—both the money kind and the energy kind. Consumers will have to pay higher electricity bills because power plant operations will be more complicated. It's harder to capture and transport CO_2 than it is to just release it into the air. The process also requires energy and a water supply. Some refer to carbon capture on coal-burning power plants as "clean coal," which is misleading. In 2020, America's only carbon capture coal plant closed down. The facility aimed to capture just 33 percent of the CO_2 it produced. It had been in operation for less than four years and shut down because it was considered too expensive. Perhaps we'd be better off investing in green energy like solar, wind, and hydro than trying to *scrub* fossil fuels clean.

DECISION TIME

Solutions to global warming exist, but they require work and sacrifice on a planetwide level. We need to come together as a species to fix the problem started by our ancestors. *(Thanks, Great-Great-Great-Great-Grandma.)* If we ignore climate change and continue contributing to it, we are risking—to put it bluntly—everything. People will lose their homes. People will go hungry. People will get sick. People will die. Not to mention the disastrous impact on non-*sapiens* species. We'll take many of them down with us.

And we may be considered the lucky generations. Our descendants will not have the same choices that are in front of us now. The goal is net-zero carbon emissions by 2050. Each year we fail to reduce our CO_2 output makes this goal more difficult—and at some point, maybe impossible. It's like wanting a big ole pumpkin for Halloween. You can't plant the seeds the week before and expect a prize-winning gourd. There's just not enough time! Right now, we still have choices. In the not-so-distant future—scientists hesitate to give an exact date—the damage to our atmosphere and planet will be irreversible. (At least, *people* won't be able to reverse the damage. Mother Nature can counter our biological attacks on her planet, but she works slowly and will take thousands, if not millions, of years. She's recovered from mass extinctions before.) It's easy to imagine future humans furious over our actions. They'll curse our names and spit on our graves because we knew better and did nothing. That's if *Homo sapiens* are still around.

This is our chance to save a species. Ourselves! We can decide to act or to suffer the consequences. Those are the only options.

HOMO SAPIENS TO-DO LIST

Here's a foolproof list to fixing global warming and human-caused climate change.

- ☐ Stop emitting greenhouse gases.
- ☐ Reduce current levels of GHGs in the atmosphere.

And here's an easy-peasy list to cutting greenhouse gases.

- ☐ Buy less stuff (AKA: reduce). That means fewer things are manufactured.
- ☐ Buy used items (AKA: reuse). That's less stuff manufactured *and* less stuff in landfills.
- ☐ Reduce, reuse, and recycle, in that order. Again, less stuff is key, and many items cannot be recycled.
- ☐ Avoid single-use plastics.
- ☐ Eat fewer animal products like meat, eggs, cheese, and eyeballs. (We've talked about this!)
- ☐ Install solar panels or a windmill.
- ☐ Get a green car. (Not the paint color, but a vehicle that doesn't guzzle gas.)
- ☐ Get a small home. Bigger houses require more energy.
- ☐ Protest climate change, which can involve skipping school. So that's fun.

☐ Stop deforestation.

☐ And also plant more trees.

☐ Learn more about science and technology.

☐ Become a scientist or engineer and directly help fix the problem.

☐ Vote! When you're old enough.

☐ Run for political office and push for laws that will save the planet.

☐ Become the head of a business and make it carbon-neutral.

☐ Organize global action on climate change.

☐ Convince others to take the threat seriously.

DEAR BRAVE READER,

We survived our terrifying look at a slew of potential disasters facing humanity. As a species, we're newbies to this planet, and if we're smart about our choices, we can continue to enjoy Earth's gifts for millennia to come. Or we can devastate the environment and even unleash war and other disasters on ourselves. We don't want to be the new neighbors who move in and destroy the community park by picking all the flowers and leaving fast-food wrappers behind. Do we?

The solutions to many of our problems require science, cooperation, and sacrifice. If we want to stop an asteroid strike, we need to see it and then defeat the threat. If we want to prevent diseases, we need to discover vaccines and treatments and then share them with the population. If we want to avoid a volcano destroying local communities and negatively influencing the world, we need better predictability and some great new technology to clean up the mess. If we want to halt global warming and climate change, we know what we need to do.

Humans are incredible, if we do say so ourselves. But, as Uncle Ben said in *Spider-Man*, "With great power comes great responsibility." *Smart man, that Uncle Ben.* The answers to our problems are ours to embrace.

The future is uncertain. (Except for the part about the sun running out of hydrogen and becoming a red giant; that's guaranteed.) Let's embrace the positive and the science. Let's use our oversized brains and commit to understanding and improving our planet. Let's make mass extinctions...well, extinct.

Thanks for reading,

Stacy

PS: I've made every attempt to deliver accurate and up-to-date scientific and historical information. (Check out the source notes; they're huge!) Still, it's possible that mistakes may have been made. My apologies. Please feel free to email me, and we can discuss any errors—assuming you're nice about it. Also, I give you permission to fix any mistakes by writing in your copy of this book. Of course, some errors may be due to timing. Science is continually changing and improving. I can write about what we understand now, but not what we might learn in the future. (Maybe I'll get to do a second edition with cool updates, like NASA discovering life on another planet!) Thank you for understanding.

ACKNOWLEDGMENTS

I've wanted to write this book for years. But when I told people about it as a potential project, some would raise their eyebrows, not quite convinced (those were the nice folks), while others just warned me that it wouldn't work. (They worried kids couldn't handle the truth.) Thankfully, there were the awesome people too—those who understood my idea, encouraged me, and helped make this book possible.

First, a big, BIG thank-you to my editor, Liz Kossnar. Her notes always pushed me further and helped me discover more. Along with spot-on suggestions, she'd write comments in the margins like "love this," or "fascinating," and my personal favorite, "This is terrifying to me." That's when I knew I had the perfect editor. I also want to thank the rest of the talented team at Little, Brown Books for Young Readers who've made me—I mean the book—look good. Megan Tingley, Jackie Engel, Alvina Ling, Jen Graham, Anna Dobbin (copy editors rock!), Patricia Alvarado, Jenny Kimura, Bill Grace, Sydney Tillman, Shawn Foster, Danielle Cantarella, and Claire Gamble.

A second big, BIG thanks to my agent, Lori Kilkelly. This book offered so many new challenges for both of us, and it came about during a *challenging* time. (We'd completed the proposal in March 2020, when the world was certainly not looking for books about human extinction.) But Lori believed in the manuscript, and in me (*she made me add that part*), and found the perfect home for *Save the People!*

Did you notice the dedication? Yep, I dedicated this book to me. More specifically, me from 2018—because this premise has haunted me since at least then. Every time I thought about starting this manuscript, I'd end up putting it aside, making excuses about being busy with other projects, which wasn't *not* true. But honestly, I was just afraid. I didn't know if I had what it took to write funny, middle-grade nonfiction. The struggle didn't end once I began. There were challenges all along the way, and I made a lot of mistakes. (Ask Liz and Lori. They're eyewitnesses.) But now you are holding my book in your hands. I did it! (With, of course, the unwavering help of all the people mentioned here.) In the future, when faced with doubts, I'm going to look back at this journey; the road to fulfilling our dreams can be bumpy. So while I wish you, dear reader, smooth travels toward your own goals, I also believe a few potholes aren't going to hold you back. Plow forward, friend! (A quick thanks to my Twitter pals for encouraging me to go forward with this unusual dedication.)

I want to acknowledge my paternal grandmother, Elizabeth "Betty" Havlik, whom I mentioned in Chapter 6. Sadly, she passed away in September 2020 at the age of ninety, just as I finished the first draft of this project. Gran had a quick wit and firm opinions. She's missed, but her spirit lives on in her children, grandchildren, great-grandchildren, and great-great-grandchildren. *Quite an impact, that Betty.*

While we're on the topic of family, I want to thank my human kids and my husband. Cora doodled initial artwork for this book, filled with science and humor, which inspired a few revisions. Someday, Cora and I will create a book together, and I have a feeling this dream will come true in the not-so-distant future. Lily and Henry read multiple drafts of the proposal and the manuscript. Their honesty about what worked and what did not work made this a better book. Lily also offered reassurances when I got frustrated. Henry helpfully challenged the validity of every scientific fact. (I exaggerate; of course not every fact. Just most.) And finally, to my husband, Brett, who listened to my ideas (and complaints) daily. This book would not exist without these four. *I love you all!*

Speed round! Thank you to Mr. Weiss, the extraordinary seventh-grade science teacher from Hanes Magnet School, for reading an early draft and offering helpful suggestions. Thank you to Dr. Stovall for answering my out-of-the-blue questions about volcanologists by email. Thank you to Nicole Miles for the earth-shattering and illuminating artwork. Thanks to Julia Sooy for recommending books on scary topics. Thanks to my writing friends for endless encouragement: Kelly Yang, Tara Luebbe, Lori Richmond, Camille Andros, Amy Cherrix (*nonfiction rules!*), and Laura Gehl. Thanks to Mom and Glen, Dad and Suzanne, Bob and Fran, and my entire extended family for all their support. *Also, Dad, I can't wait for you to read this! I know you love nonfiction—at least nonfiction about history—so I hope you enjoy some science-y nonfiction written by one of your favorite daughters.*

Stay with me; I'm almost done. I've never been one for short acknowledgments. I have to mention my furry babies. Day to day, "Ray-ka," Munchkin, and Luigi play a significant role in my writing life. That's because we all *share* a home office. They offer no commentary on the manuscript, but their presence makes my life better. *Woof!*

Thank you to Lin-Manuel Miranda, who had nothing to do with this book beyond the impact of his creativity and positivity. I've acknowledged Mr. Miranda in all three of my novels, and I will continue to thank him in all books until he notices—and maybe after too.

The final thank-you is for you, reader. Thanks for picking up this book and sharing your time with me. *Now, go save the world!*

SOME WORDS THAT MIGHT NEED EXPLAINING

amoeba: a type of single-celled organism

anthropogenic: influenced or caused by human activity, especially on nature

antibiotic: a medicine used against bacterial infections and diseases

archeologist: a person who studies ancient humans or ancient history

atom: smallest form of matter; has neutrons, protons, and electrons

bacterium: a single-celled organism that can be helpful (like the kind in our gut) or harmful (like the kind that causes disease)

binary star system: a solar system with two suns

black hole: a place in the universe where gravity is so strong that not even light can escape

carrion: a dead, decaying animal

exoplanet: a planet not in our solar system

extinction: the death of an entire species

fauna: animals

fission: an atom breaking apart; creates a lot of energy

flora: plants

food insecurity: a lack of food on a consistent basis

fossil: preserved evidence of ancient life

fusion: two atoms coming together; creates a lot of energy

gamma-ray burst: strongest known explosion of energy and light; possibly created as a black hole forms

Gondwana: ancient continent consisting of modern-day Africa, South America, Antarctica, and Australia

habitable: suitable for living

hemorrhaging: bleeding; often refers to uncontrolled bleeding

human: a primate of the genus *Homo*; includes you

hypothesis: a suggested explanation or solution

immunity: the ability to resist an infection or disease

invertebrate: an animal without a backbone

Laurentia: ancient continent of which North America was part

mass extinction: when at least 75 percent of flora and fauna go extinct

megafauna: ginormous animals, like mammoths

millennia: thousands of years

millennium: 1,000 years

multi-star system: solar system with two or more suns

nebula: a space cloud made of dust and gas

net zero: in and out are equal; often refers to CO_2 emissions

nomad: person without a fixed place to live; instead they move around or roam

non-avian dinosaur: any dinosaur that's not a bird

ozone: O_3, a gas; the ozone layer in the atmosphere reduces the amount of harmful ultraviolet rays that reach Earth's surface

Panthalassa: the enormous prehistoric ocean

parasite: an organism that lives off another organism

pathogen: a disease-causing microorganism

porous: having lots of holes or gaps

proto: early or first (used in combination with another word)

solar flare: a sudden release of energy from a region of the sun

sunspot: a huge, dark, cool area on the surface of the sun

supervolcano: large volcanic eruption that measures an eight on the VEI scale; not a science-approved term

tetrapod: an animal with vertebrae and four limbs; includes amphibians, reptiles, birds, and mammals

TNT: an explosive compound

tsunami: a huge sea wave (or waves) caused by a disturbance like an earthquake or volcano

vaccination: treatment used to create immunity

variolation: obsolete treatment to create immunity to smallpox; a patient was exposed to the disease through their nose or a cut

virus: an infectious agent that must enter a cell to multiply and spread

SELECTED BIBLIOGRAPHY

BOOKS

Berman, Bob. *Earth-Shattering: Violent Supernovas, Galactic Explosions, Biological Mayhem, Nuclear Meltdowns, and Other Hazards to Life in Our Universe.* Little, Brown, 2019.

Brannen, Peter. *The Ends of the World: Volcanic Apocalypses, Lethal Oceans, and Our Quest to Understand Earth's Past Mass Extinctions.* HarperCollins, 2017.

Brusatte, Steve. *The Rise and Fall of the Dinosaurs: A New History of a Lost World.* HarperCollins, 2018.

Christian, David. *Origin Story: A Big History of Everything.* Penguin Books, 2019.

Foer, Jonathan Safran. *We Are the Weather: Saving the Planet Begins at Breakfast.* Farrar, Straus and Giroux, 2019.

Frank, Adam. *Light of the Stars: Alien Worlds and the Fate of the Earth.* W. W. Norton, 2019.

Harari, Yuval Noah. *Sapiens: A Brief History of Humankind.* Harper Perennial, 2018.

Hazen, Robert M. *The Story of Earth: The First 4.5 Billion Years, from Stardust to Living Planet.* Penguin Books, 2012.

Newman, Lenore. *Lost Feast: Culinary Extinction and the Future of Food.* ECW Press, 2019.

Prothero, Donald R. *When Humans Nearly Vanished: The Catastrophic Explosion of the Toba Volcano.* Smithsonian Books, 2018.

Wallace-Wells, David. *The Uninhabitable Earth: Life after Warming.* Penguin Random House, 2020.

Walsh, Bryan. *End Times: A Brief Guide to the End of the World: Asteroids, Super Volcanoes, Rogue Robots, and More.* Seven Dials, 2019.

ONLINE

Betz, Eric. "Here's What Happens to the Solar System When the Sun Dies." *Discover Magazine*, February 6, 2020. www.discovermagazine .com/the-sciences/heres-what-happens-to-the-solar-system-when -the-sun-dies.

Byrd, Deborah. "Today in Science: The Chelyabinsk Meteor." *EarthSky*, February 15, 2019. https://earthsky.org/space/meteor-asteroid -chelyabinsk-russia-feb-15-2013.

"COVID-19 Dashboard." Coronavirus Resource Center, Johns Hopkins University. https://coronavirus.jhu.edu/map.html.

Encyclopedia Britannica. "Drake Equation." Updated April 26, 2020. www.britannica.com/science/Drake-equation.

Greshko, Michael. "What Are Mass Extinctions, and What Causes Them?" *National Geographic*, September 26, 2019. www.nationalgeo graphic.com/science/article/mass-extinction.

Intergovernmental Panel on Climate Change. *Special Report: Global Warming of 1.5 °C.* www.ipcc.ch/sr15.

Kornei, Katherine. "A New Timeline of the Day the Dinosaurs Began to Die Out." *New York Times*, September 10, 2019. www.nytimes .com/2019/09/10/science/chicxulub-asteroid-impact-dinosaurs.html.

Plantrician Project. "Food Math 101." https://plantricianproject.org/food -math-101.

Plumer, Brad, and Nadja Popovich. "Why Half a Degree of Global Warm- ing Is a Big Deal." *New York Times*, October 7, 2018. www.nytimes .com/interactive/2018/10/07/climate/ipcc-report-half-degree.html.

Rothman, Lily. "After the Bomb: Survivors of the Atomic Blasts in Hiroshima and Nagasaki Share Their Stories." *Time*. https://time.com/after-the-bomb.

Smithsonian National Museum of Natural History. "What does it mean to be human?" https://humanorigins.si.edu.

Wei-Haas, Maya. "How Dangerous Are Supervolcanoes? Get the Facts." *National Geographic*, March 19, 2019. www.nationalgeographic.com/science/article/supervolcano-yellowstone.

SOURCE NOTES

PART I

3   "Those who fail": Winston Churchill, quoted in Laurence Geller, "Folger Library—Churchill's Shakespeare," International Churchill Society, http://winstonchurchill.org/resources/in-the-media/churchill-in-the-news/folger-library-churchills-shakespeare.

CHAPTER 1

5   Once upon a time: David Christian, *Origin Story: A Big History of Everything* (Penguin Books, 2019), page 21.

5   About 180 million: Mike Wall, "Astronomers Glimpse Signposts of Universe's First Stars," *Scientific American*, February 28, 2018, www.scientificamerican.com/article/astronomers-glimpse-signposts-of-universe-rsquo-s-first-stars.

5   Our neighborhood star: Christian, *Origin Story*, page 62.

6   The leftover dust and gas: National Aeronautics and Space Administration (NASA), "Our Solar System," https://solarsystem.nasa.gov/solar-system/our-solar-system/in-depth.

6   when a Mars-sized rock: NASA, "About the Moon," https://moon.nasa.gov/about/in-depth.

7   Then things cooled off: Robert M. Hazen, *The Story of Earth: The First 4.5 Billion Years, from Stardust to Living Planet* (Viking, 2012), chapter 4.

7   microscopic life that existed 3.5 billion years ago: Hazen, *Story of Earth*, page 149.

7   Finally, oxygen!: David Biello, "The Origin of Oxygen in Earth's Atmosphere," *Scientific American*, August 19, 2009, www.scientificamerican.com/article/origin-of-oxygen-in-atmosphere.

7   the Boring Billion: Peter Brannen, *The Ends of the World: Volcanic Apocalypses, Lethal Oceans, and Our Quest to Understand Earth's Past Mass Extinctions* (HarperCollins, 2017), page 15.

8   Ice covered the globe: Brannen, *Ends of the World*, page 16.

8   Things got exciting: *Encyclopedia Britannica*, "Cambrian Explosion," updated August 8, 2019, www.britannica.com/science/Cambrian-explosion; Brannen, *Ends of the World*, page 17.

8   The dates of mass extinctions are from Michael Greshko, "What Are Mass Extinctions, and What Causes Them?," *National Geographic*, September 26, 2019, www.nationalgeographic.com/science/article/mass-extinction.

9   The first dinosaurs scampered: Steve Brusatte, *The Rise and Fall of the Dinosaurs: A New History of a Lost World* (HarperCollins, 2018), page 37.

9   *Homo erectus* (translation: upright man): Yuval Noah Harari, *Sapiens: A Brief History of Humankind* (Harper Perennial, 2018), page 5.

10   Your great-great-great: Ewen Callaway, "Oldest *Homo sapiens* Fossil Claim Rewrites Our Species' History," *Nature*, June 7, 2017, www.nature.com/news /oldest-homo-sapiens-fossil-claim-rewrites-our-species-history-1.22114.

10   Until 12,000 years ago...farming: Harari, *Sapiens*, page 42.

10   Johannes Gutenberg invented: *Encyclopedia Britannica*, "Printing Press," updated November 25, 2019, www.britannica.com/technology/printing-press.

10   Pi Sheng created: *Encyclopedia Britannica*, "Printing," updated October 1, 2020, www.britannica.com/topic/printing-publishing/History-of-printing.

11   The first industrial revolution: *Encyclopedia Britannica*, "Industrial Revolution," updated May 21, 2021, www.britannica.com/event/Industrial-Revolution.

11   Humans made the first nuclear bomb: *Encyclopedia Britannica*, "Atomic Bomb," updated August 27, 2020, www.britannica.com/technology/atomic-bomb.

11   On July 20, 1969: NASA, "Exploration," http://moon.nasa.gov/exploration /history.

11   NASA hopes to send astronauts: NASA, "Moon to Mars Overview," www.nasa .gov/topics/moon-to-mars/overview.

12   about 7.9 billion *Homo sapiens*: "World Population Dashboard," accessed September 16, 2021, www. unfpa.org/data/world-population-dashboard.

13   Our little turf exists: *Encyclopedia Britannica*, "Milky Way Galaxy," updated October 13, 2020, www.britannica.com/place/Milky-Way-Galaxy.

13   99.9 percent of your DNA: Catherine Zuckerman, "DNA, Explained," *National Geographic*, February 26, 2019, www.nationalgeographic.com/science/article /dna-deoxyribonucleic-acid.

CHAPTER 2

14   75 percent of all species are terminated: Frédérik Saltré and Corey J. A. Bradshaw, "What Is a 'Mass Extinction' and Are We in One Now?," *The Conversation*, November 12, 2019, https://theconversation.com/what-is-a-mass -extinction-and-are-we-in-one-now-122535.

14   85% of species croaked: Michael Greshko, "What Are Mass Extinctions, and What Causes Them?," *National Geographic*, September 26, 2019, www.national geographic.com/science/article/mass-extinction.

14   70–80% of all animal species...non-avian dinosaurs: *Encyclopedia Britannica*, "Extinction," updated March 31, 2021, www.britannica.com/science /extinction-biology.

15   at least 10,000 years old: *National Geographic Encyclopedia*, "Fossil," updated February 22, 2013, www.nationalgeographic.org/encyclopedia/fossil.

16   Silver Medal! The Second Worst: *Encyclopedia Britannica*, "Extinction."

16   This is the time of the "sea without fish": Peter Brannen, *The Ends of the World: Volcanic Apocalypses, Lethal Oceans, and Our Quest to Understand Earth's Past Mass Extinctions* (HarperCollins, 2017), pages 26–27.

16   Earth's sea levels...barren: Brannen, *Ends of the World*, pages 31–33.

17   king of the continents...Laurentia: "Ordovician Period," *National Geographic*, www.nationalgeographic.com/science/article/ordovician.

17   The Panthalassic Ocean...globe: *Encyclopedia Britannica*, "Ordovician Period," updated February 11, 2021, www.britannica.com/science/Ordovician-Period.

17   The sun was 3 to 5 percent less bright: L. Robin M. Cocks and Trond H. Torsvik, "Ordovician Palaeogeography and Climate Change," *Gondwana Research* (2020), https://doi.org/10.1016/j.gr.2020.09.008.

17   Earth rotated faster...hours: Brannen, *Ends of the World*, page 33.

17   The air had more carbon...temperatures: *Encyclopedia Britannica*, "Ordovician Period."

17   The last centuries...extinction: Brannen, *Ends of the World*, page 37.

18   Gondwana drifted to...continents: *Encyclopedia Britannica*, "Ordovician-Silurian Extinction," updated June 1, 2020, www.britannica.com/science/Ordovician-Silurian-extinction.

18   the new Appalachian...air: Brannen, *Ends of the World*, page 52.

18   Take rocks...limestone: Paul Voosen, "Rise of Carbon Dioxide–Absorbing Mountains in Tropics May Set Thermostat for Global Climate," *Science*, December 28, 2018, www.sciencemag.org/news/2018/12/rise-carbon-dioxide-absorbing-mountains-tropics-may-set-thermostat-global-climate.

18   The general rule: The more CO_2: National Oceanic and Atmospheric Administration (NOAA), "Temperature Change and Carbon Dioxide Change," www.ncdc.noaa.gov/global-warming/temperature-change.

19   Some species of brachiopods...of trilobites: Greshko, "What Are Mass Extinctions."

19   the *Isotelus rex*: Brannen, *Ends of the World*, page 28.

19   One fossilized *I. rex*: David M. Rudkin, Graham A. Young, Robert J. Elias, and Edward P. Dobrzanski, "The World's Biggest Trilobite—*Isotelus rex* New Species from the Upper Ordovician of Northern Manitoba, Canada," *Journal of Paleontology* 77, no. 1 (2003): 99–112, https://doi.org/10.1017/S0022336000043456.

19   The Fifth and Least Impressive: *Encyclopedia Britannica*, "Extinction."

19   Now we travel...period: Brannen, *Ends of the World*, page 68.

20   grow to thirty feet long: Bob Strauss, "Dunkleosteus," ThoughtCo, January 16, 2020, www.thoughtco.com/overview-of-dunkleosteus-1093659.

20   A third of its body size: John Mangels, "My, What a Big Mouth You Have: Studying *Dunkleosteus'* Jaws and the Injuries They Inflicted Provide Clues to a Violent Lifestyle," Cleveland Museum of Natural History, January 6, 2017, www.cmnh.org/dunkjaws.

20   because *Dunkleosteus* could open...cages: Brannen, *Ends of the World*, pages 88–89.

20   the world became a home for tetrapods: *Encyclopedia Britannica*, "Devonian Period," updated May 3, 2021, www.britannica.com/science/Devonian-Period.

20   Earth had proto-trees: Brannen, *Ends of the World*, page 75.

20   Later came a 100-foot-tall tree: Brannen, *Ends of the World*, page 78.

20   This was a long...359 million years ago: Brannen, *Ends of the World*, pages 69–70.

21   over 3 million square miles of the world's reefs: Brannen, *Ends of the World*, page 69.

21   The second punch: Brannen, *Ends of the World*, pages 97–99.

22   Our scary friend *Dunkleosteus*: Strauss, "Dunkleosteus."

22   More species of trilobites...coral: *Encyclopedia Britannica*, "Devonian Period."

22   *We're Number One!*: *Encyclopedia Britannica*, "Extinction."

22   the 11.5-foot-long *Dimetrodon*: *Encyclopedia Britannica*, "Dimetrodon," updated October 17, 2018, www.britannica.com/animal/Dimetrodon.

22   This was also...Panthalassa: Brannen, *Ends of the World*, page 119.

22   but no grasses or flowers yet: Brannen, *Ends of the World*, page 118.

22   The greatest mass extinction...half mile deep: Brannen, *Ends of the World*, pages 123–24.

23   Pangea could have reached 140°F: Brannen, *Ends of the World*, page 127.

23   The world became a hothouse...insects: Greshko, "What Are Mass Extinctions."

23   The ocean warmed...shell: Brannen, *Ends of the World*, pages 129–30.

23   The rest of the placoderms...*Moschops*: *Encyclopedia Britannica*, "Permian Extinction," updated February 1, 2021, www.britannica.com/science/Permian-extinction.

23   The largest insect ever, *Meganeuropsis*: Vasika Udurawane, "The Biggest Insect Ever Was a Huge 'Dragonfly,'" *Earth Archives*, https://eartharchives.org/articles/the-biggest-insect-ever-was-a-huge-dragonfly/index.html.

24   Our not-a-dino friend *Dimetrodon*: *Encyclopedia Britannica*, "Dimetrodon."

24   The rest of the trilobites: Brannen, *Ends of the World*, page 107.

24   95 percent of all marine species and 70 percent of land species: *Encyclopedia Britannica*, "Permian Extinction."

24   Number Four: *Encyclopedia Britannica*, "Extinction."

24   Trees missed out on the first 10 million years: Brannen, *Ends of the World*, page 142.

24   The Early Triassic...equator: Brannen, *Ends of the World*, pages 143–44.

24   when croc-like beings dominated: Brannen, *Ends of the World*, page 145.

24   One breed of rauisuchian…ate little dinosaurs: Eleanor Imster, "These Giant Croc-Like Carnivores Terrorized Triassic Dinosaurs," *EarthSky*, October 2, 2019, https://earthsky.org/earth/extinct-giant-croclike-carnivores -triassic-rauisuchian.

25   The Triassic gave Earth its first dinosaurs: Brannen, *Ends of the World*, page 145.

25   Mammals arrived…rat-sized: Bob Strauss, "The Evolution of the First Mammals," ThoughtCo, June 24, 2019, www.thoughtco.com/the-first-mammals -1093311.

25   The planet also welcomed…pterosaurs: *Encyclopedia Britannica*, "Pterosaur," updated April 2, 2020, www.britannica.com/animal/pterosaur.

25   Toward the end…North America: Brannen, *Ends of the World*, page 149.

25   The first ichthyosaurs…seas: Brannen, *Ends of the World*, page 143.

25   Pangea split apart: Brannen, *Ends of the World*, page 152.

25   Volcanic activity went into overdrive: Greshko, "What Are Mass Extinctions."

25   Geologists see evidence…Morocco: Brannen, *Ends of the World*, page 154.

26   Conodonts, which are small marine invertebrates: Gemma Tarlach, "The Five Mass Extinctions That Have Swept Our Planet," *Discover Magazine*, July 18, 2018, www.discovermagazine.com/the-sciences/mass-extinctions.

26   The enormous croc-like rauisuchians: Imster, "Giant Croc-Like Carnivores."

26   other large crocodilians: Greshko, "What Are Mass Extinctions."

26   The dolphin-like ichthyosaurs: Brannen, *Ends of the World*, page 160.

26   Coral reefs almost go entirely extinct: Brannen, *Ends of the World*, page 161.

CHAPTER 3

27   It's also known…C-Pg: *Encyclopedia Britannica*, "K–T Extinction," updated May 21, 2020, www.britannica.com/science/K-T-extinction.

28   Dinosaurs and mammals…Great Dying: "Triassic Period," *National Geographic*, www.nationalgeographic.com/science/article/triassic.

28   *Repenomamus*, actually ate small (or dead) dinosaurs: Riley Black, "When Mammals Ate Dinosaurs," *Smithsonian Magazine*, June 20, 2012, www.smithsonian mag.com/science-nature/when-mammals-ate-dinosaurs-129282708.

28   about the size of a crow: *Encyclopedia Britannica*, "Dromaeosaur," updated January 27, 2011, www.britannica.com/animal/dromaeosaur.

28   *Spinosaurus*, went extinct approximately 94 million years ago: *Encyclopedia Britannica*, "Spinosaurus," updated October 24, 2018, www.britannica.com /animal/Spinosaurus.

28   "king of the tyrant lizards"…ago: Amy McKeever, "Why Tyrannosaurus rex Was One of the Fiercest Predators of All Time," *National Geographic*, www .nationalgeographic.com/animals/facts/tyrannosaurus-rex.

28   the stegosauruses, which went belly-up: *Encyclopedia Britannica*, "Stegosaurus,"
      updated December 12, 2019, www.britannica.com/animal/Stegosaurus.

29   Earth's Worst Day: Steve Brusatte, *The Rise and Fall of the Dinosaurs: A New History of a Lost World* (HarperCollins, 2018), pages 309–19.

34   The summary of the Alvarezes' asteroid-impact theory is from Brusatte, *Rise and Fall*, pages 323–26.

34   Finally, in 1991...created it: Charles Q. Choi, "Chicxulub Asteroid Impact: The Dino-Killer That Scientists Laughed At," Space.com, February 7, 2013, www.space.com/19681-dinosaur-killing-asteroid-chicxulub-crater.html.

35   the impact 212 million years ago...crater: National Aeronautics and Space Administration (NASA), "Manicouagan Impact Structure, Quebec," June 1, 2001, https://earthobservatory.nasa.gov/images/1993/manicouagan-impact-structure-quebec.

35   That help could have come from...planet: Paul Voosen, "Did Volcanic Eruptions Help Kill Off the Dinosaurs?," *Science*, February 21, 2019, www.sciencemag.org/news/2019/02/did-volcanic-eruptions-help-kill-dinosaurs.

36   Not all dinosaurs are extinct...tyrannosaurs: Victoria Jaggard, "These Are the Dinosaurs That Didn't Die," *National Geographic*, May 2018, www.nationalgeographic.com/magazine/article/dinosaurs-survivors-birds-fossils.

36   Scientists began searching...1859: Matt Kaplan, "*Archaeopteryx* No Longer First Bird," *Nature*, July 27, 2011, www.nature.com/news/2011/110727/full/news.2011.443.html.

36   Evolution is the theory: *Encyclopedia Britannica*, "Evolution," updated May 27, 2021, www.britannica.com/science/evolution-scientific-theory.

36   *Archaeopteryx* had feathered wings: John Nudds, "How We Discovered a New Species of the 'Missing Link' between Dinosaurs and Birds," *The Conversation*, October 24, 2018, https://theconversation.com/how-we-discovered-a-new-species-of-the-missing-link-between-dinosaurs-and-birds-102363.

36   But as more fossils...beast: Emily Singer, "How Dinosaurs Shrank and Became Birds," *Scientific American*, June 12, 2015, www.scientificamerican.com/article/how-dinosaurs-shrank-and-became-birds.

37   *Glyptodon*, a mammal similar to an armadillo: *Encyclopedia Britannica*, "Glyptodon," updated October 12, 2018, www.britannica.com/animal/Glyptodon.

37   *Megatherium*, better known as: *Encyclopedia Britannica*, "Megatherium," updated October 10, 2018, www.britannica.com/animal/Megatherium.

37   *Daeodon*, or "terrible pig": Bob Strauss, "Daeodon, Formerly Known as Dinohyus, the Terrible Pig," ThoughtCo, January 16, 2020, www.thoughtco.com/daeodon-dinohyus-terrible-pig-1093187.

CHAPTER 4

38   *Homo* is Latin...wise: *Encyclopedia Britannica*, "Homo sapiens," updated November 12, 2020, www.britannica.com/topic/Homo-sapiens.

38   a human is an animal under the genus *Homo*: *Encyclopedia Britannica*, "Human Being," updated February 2, 2018, www.britannica.com/topic/human-being.

38   This includes *Homo sapiens, Homo erectus*: *Encyclopedia Britannica*, "Human Evolution," updated January 12, 2021, www.britannica.com/science /human-evolution.

38   *Homo floresiensis...size: Encyclopedia Britannica*, "Homo floresiensis," updated April 7, 2020, www.britannica.com/topic/Homo-floresiensis.

38   and Neanderthals: *Encyclopedia Britannica*, "Human Evolution."

38   The chimpanzee and the bonobo...*Pan*: "Genetic Evidence," Human Origins Program, Smithsonian Institution, updated October 27, 2020, https://human origins.si.edu/evidence/genetics.

38   It's our big...8 percent: Yuval Noah Harari, *Sapiens: A Brief History of Humankind* (Harper Perennial, 2018), page 9.

39   Current evidence points...ago: Laura Geggel, "First 'Homo' Species Left Africa with Ape-Like Brains," *Live Science*, April 8, 2021, www.livescience.com /human-brain-evolution.html.

39   *Homo sapiens* scientific classification is from *New World Encyclopedia*, "Homo (Genus)," www.newworldencyclopedia.org/entry/Homo_(genus).

39   *Homo neanderthalensis* scientific classification is from *New World Encyclopedia*, "Neanderthal," www.newworldencyclopedia.org/entry/Neanderthal.

39   *Pan troglodytes* scientific classification is from *New World Encyclopedia*, "Chimpanzee," www.newworldencyclopedia.org/entry/Chimpanzee.

40   In 1974...fossils: *Encyclopedia Britannica*, "Lucy," updated May 15, 2013, www .britannica.com/topic/Lucy-fossil.

40   They named the specimen...find: Arizona State University Institute of Human Origins, "Lucy's Story," October 19, 2020, https://iho.asu.edu/about /lucys-story.

40   *Australopithecus afarensis*: *Encyclopedia Britannica*, "Lucy."

40   Lucy is 3.2 million...two legs: *Encyclopedia Britannica*, "Lucy."

40   The first *Homo* species...mystery: *Encyclopedia Britannica*, "Homo erectus," updated November 13, 2020, www.britannica.com/topic/Homo-erectus.

41   There's no evidence...slightly: Paul Rincon, "Homo erectus: Ancient Humans Survived Longer Than We Thought," *BBC News*, December 18, 2019, www.bbc .com/news/science-environment-50827603.

41   Triceratops roamed for 3 million years: *Encyclopedia Britannica*, "Triceratops," updated February 19, 2021, www.britannica.com/animal/Triceratops.

41   Blue whales...1.5 million years: Tim Vernimmen, "Fossil of 85-Foot Blue Whale Is Largest Ever Discovered," *National Geographic*, April 30, 2019, www.nationalgeographic.com/science/article/largest-fossil-blue-whale -found-italy-paleontology.

41   *H. erectus* hunted…2 million years: Brian Handwerk, "Fossils from Some of the Last Homo erectus Hint at the End of the Long-Lived Species," *Smithsonian Magazine*, December 18, 2019, www.smithsonianmag.com/science-nature /fossils-some-last-homo-erectus-hint-end-long-lived-species-180973816.

41   Like other species…debate: John P. Rafferty, "Just How Old Is *Homo sapiens*?," *Encyclopedia Britannica*, www.britannica.com/story/just-how-old-is-homo -sapiens.

41   About 90,000 years ago…Eurasia: Amanda Mascarelli, "Climate Swings Drove Patterns of Early Human Migration," *Sapiens*, November 5, 2018, www.sapiens .org/biology/early-human-migration.

42   Neanderthals shared the planet…Asia: *Encyclopedia Britannica*, "Neanderthal," updated February 6, 2020, www.britannica.com/topic/Neanderthal.

42   had bigger brains than *H. sapiens*: Bridget Alex, "Neanderthal Brains: Bigger, Not Necessarily Better," *Discover Magazine*, September 21, 2018, www.discovermag azine.com/planet-earth/neanderthal-brains-bigger-not-necessarily-better.

42   That's not accurate…not human: Jon Mooallem, "Neanderthals Were People, Too," *New York Times Magazine*, January 11, 2017, www.nytimes.com/2017/01/11 /magazine/neanderthals-were-people-too.html.

42   Neanderthals had muscular arms…chests: *Encyclopedia Britannica*, "Neanderthal."

42   They painted!…65,000 years ago: Michael Greshko, "World's Oldest Cave Art Found—and Neanderthals Made It," *National Geographic*, February 22, 2018, www.nationalgeographic.com/science/article/neanderthals-cave-art-humans -evolution-science.

42   If a family member…religious practices: *Encyclopedia Britannica*, "Neanderthal."

43   No More Neanderthals: Harari, *Sapiens*, pages 14–19.

43   disappeared between 35,000 and 24,000 years ago: *Encyclopedia Britannica*, "Neanderthal."

44   Our ancestors probably…marrow: Harari, *Sapiens*, page 11.

44   Crows fashion twigs…food: Douglas Main, "Like Chess Players, These Crows Can Plan Several Steps Ahead," *National Geographic*, February 7, 2019, www.nationalgeographic.com/animals/article/new-caledonian-crows-plan -ahead-with-tools.

44   Elephants use branches as fly swatters: Shimon Shuchat, "Weapons, Ear Cleaners, and Fly Swatters: Elephant Tool Use," Medium, April 23, 2018, https:// medium.com/elp-rumbles/weapons-ear-cleaners-and-fly-swatters-elephant -tool-use-574ed7a16e48.

44   And chimpanzees create…weapons: Ed Yong, "Chimpanzees Make Spears to Hunt Bushbabies," *National Geographic*, October 15, 2008, www.nationalgeographic .com/science/article/chimpanzees-make-spears-to-hunt-bushbabies.

45   fire's real advantage…mastered the flame: Harari, *Sapiens*, pages 12–13.

45   maybe as far back as 1.5 million years ago: Andrew C. Scott, "When Did Humans Discover Fire? The Answer Depends on What You Mean by 'Discover,'" *Time*, June 1, 2018, https://time.com/5295907/discover-fire.

45 The real reason...language: Harari, *Sapiens*, page 19.

47 it was a genetic mutation in *H. sapiens*: Harari, *Sapiens*, pages 21–25.

49 The first non-nomadic...holes: Harari, *Sapiens*, page 48.

49 An ancient farmer's...varied: Harari, *Sapiens*, page 79.

49 Farming led to inequality: Erin Blakemore, "What Was the Neolithic Revolution?," *National Geographic*, April 5, 2019, www.nationalgeographic.com /culture/article/neolithic-agricultural-revolution.

50 11 billion strong by 2100: United Nations Department of Economic and Social Affairs, "Growing at a Slower Pace, World Population Is Expected to Reach 9.7 Billion in 2050 and Could Peak at Nearly 11 Billion around 2100," June 17, 2019, www.un.org/development/desa/en/news/population/world-population -prospects-2019.html.

CHAPTER 5

51 *H. sapiens* went through...ago: Michael R. Rampino and Stanley H. Ambrose, "Volcanic Winter in the Garden of Eden: The Toba Supereruption and the Late Pleistocene Human Population Crash" (2000), https: //nyuscholars.nyu.edu/en/publications/volcanic-winter-in-the-garden-of -eden-the-toba-supereruption-and-.

51 As our ancestors moved out of Africa: Ann Gibbons, "How We Lost Our Diversity," *Science*, October 8, 2009, www.sciencemag.org/news/2009/10/how -we-lost-our-diversity.

51 3,000 and 10,000 individuals: Rampino and Ambrose, "Volcanic Winter."

52 DNA, they would be 99.9 percent identical: National Human Genome Research Institute, "Genetics vs. Genomics Fact Sheet," updated September 7, 2018, www.genome.gov/about-genomics/fact-sheets/Genetics-vs-Genomics.

52 Approximately 74,000 years...lid: "Ancient Supervolcano Affected the Ends of the Earth," *Live Science*, November 5, 2012, www.livescience.com/24547-toba -volcano-ice-cores.html.

52 it was the most massive...years: "Ancient Supervolcano."

52 eruption cloud reaching nineteen miles high: Bryan Walsh, *End Times: A Brief Guide to the End of the World: Asteroids, Super Volcanoes, Rogue Robots, and More* (Seven Dials, 2019), page 59.

52 airplanes fly five to seven miles: Celine Hacobian, "Here's How High Planes Actually Fly, According to Experts," *Time*, June 27, 2018, https://time .com/5309905/how-high-do-planes-fly.

53 The flowing lava...hour: Walsh, *End Times*, page 58.

53 A layer of soot...places: David Bressan, "Most Powerful Supervolcano Eruption in the Last 28 Million Years Had No Effect on Human Evolution," *Forbes*, February 26, 2020, www.forbes.com/sites/davidbressan/2020/02/26/most -powerful-supervolcano-eruption-in-the-last-28-million-years-had-no-effect -on-human-evolution.

53   Another ejected material…rain: "Ancient Supervolcano."

54   One sample "went back" 2.7 million years: Paul Voosen, "Record-Shattering 2.7-Million-Year-Old Ice Core Reveals Start of the Ice Ages," *Science*, August 15, 2017, www.sciencemag.org/news/2017/08/record-shattering-27-million-year -old-ice-core-reveals-start-ice-ages.

54   Using an ice core…measurements: Walsh, *End Times*, page 60.

55   some estimates say by as much as 18°F: Walsh, *End Times*, page 60.

55   When scientists examined…ash: "Ancient Supervolcano."

56   new studies suggest…time: "Ancient Supervolcano."

56   Researchers working at Pinnacle Point: Michael Greshko, "These Ancient Humans Survived a Supervolcano," *National Geographic*, March 12, 2018, www.nationalgeographic.com/science/article/toba-supervolcano-eruption -humans-south-africa-science.

56   Closer to the eruption…supervolcano: Chris Clarkson and Michael Petraglia, "Stone Tools Show Humans in India Survived the Cataclysmic Toba Eruption 74,000 Years Ago," *The Conversation*, February 25, 2020, https://theconversation .com/stone-tools-show-humans-in-india-survived-the-cataclysmic-toba -eruption-74-000-years-ago-132101.

PART II

59   It's estimated 99 percent…gone: Michael Greshko, "What Are Mass Extinc-tions, and What Causes Them?," *National Geographic*, September 26, 2019, www .nationalgeographic.com/science/article/mass-extinction.

CHAPTER 6

61   Earth is pelted…day: National Aeronautics and Space Administration (NASA), "Asteroid Fast Facts," updated August 7, 2017, www.nasa.gov/mission_pages /asteroids/overview/fastfacts.html.

62   Most asteroids are…ago: NASA, "Asteroids," https://solarsystem.nasa.gov /asteroids-comets-and-meteors/asteroids/in-depth.

62   In 1998, Congress told…decade: NASA, "NASA's Search for Asteroids to Help Protect Earth and Understand Our History," April 22, 2014, www.nasa.gov /content/nasas-search-for-asteroids-to-help-protect-earth-and-understand -our-history.

62   exceeded that goal and found 95 percent: NASA, "Twenty Years of Tracking Near-Earth Objects," July 23, 2018, www.jpl.nasa.gov/news/twenty-years-of -tracking-near-earth-objects.

62   They're calculating the path…100 years: According to the available data in May 2021, no asteroids are threatening Earth. See NASA, "Sentry: Earth Impact Monitoring," https://cneos.jpl.nasa.gov/sentry.

63   Things from Space: NASA, "Asteroid or Meteor: What's the Difference?," updated March 30, 2021, https://spaceplace.nasa.gov/asteroid-or-meteor/en.

64   Since our world is 71 percent ocean: *Encyclopedia Britannica*, "Ocean," updated May 7, 2021, www.britannica.com/ science/ocean.

64   A watery crash…tsunamis: Nola Taylor Redd, "New Asteroid Study Suggests Hollywood Is Wrong about Ocean Impacts," *NBC News*, April 17, 2017, www .nbcnews.com/mach/space/new-asteroid-study-suggests-hollywood-wrong -about-ocean-impacts-n747321.

64   ten times more destructive: "Hazardous Asteroid Effects Ranked from Least to Most Destructive," *ScienceDaily*, April 19, 2017, www.sciencedaily.com/releases /2017/04/170419122015.htm.

65   Only about 3 percent…populated: United Nations, "Goal 11: Make Cities Inclusive, Safe, Resilient and Sustainable," UN Sustainable Development Goals, www.un.org/sustainabledevelopment/cities.

65   The wind and shock…hour: Doyle Rice, "1,000-mph Winds, Shock Waves Deadliest Effects of Asteroid Strike," *USA Today*, April 19, 2017, www .usatoday.com/story/tech/sciencefair/2017/04/19/asteroid-strike-deadliest -hazards/100652436.

65   forty to forty-five miles per hour: John Perritano, "Yes, Wind Can Blow You Away If It's the Right Speed," HowStuffWorks, March 16, 2017, https://science .howstuffworks.com/nature/climate-weather/atmospheric/wind-can-blow -you-away-right-speed.htm.

67   The date was…Russia: Deborah Byrd, "Today in Science: The Chelyabinsk Meteor," *EarthSky*, February 15, 2019, https://earthsky.org/space /meteor-asteroid-chelyabinsk-russia-feb-15-2013.

67   Over a thousand…treatment: *National Geographic Encyclopedia*, "Meteor," updated August 1, 2014, https://staging.nationalgeographic.org/encyclopedia /meteor.

67   Scientists estimate the…across: Byrd, "Today in Science."

67   Most of it broke…city: NASA, "Five Years after the Chelyabinsk Meteor: NASA Leads Efforts in Planetary Defense," February 15, 2018, www.nasa.gov/feature /five-years-after-the-chelyabinsk-meteor-nasa-leads-efforts-in-planetary -defense.

67   The largest remaining chunk…lake: Byrd, "Today in Science."

68   On this day…of our planet: Deborah Byrd, "Chelyabinsk Meteor Mystery 3 Years Later," *EarthSky*, February 15, 2016, https://earthsky.org/space /chelyabinsk-meteor-mystery-3-years-later.

68   the Chelyabinsk rock…of the sun: Alan Boyle, "Russian Meteor's Terrifying Trek Detailed in New Studies," *NBC News*, November 6, 2013, www .nbcnews.com/sciencemain/russian-meteors-terrifying-trek-detailed-new -studies-8c11542598.

68 a meteorite killing one man: Michelle Starr, "We Have the First-Ever Credible Evidence of Someone Killed by a Falling Meteorite," *ScienceAlert*, April 24, 2020, www.sciencealert.com/we-finally-have-credible-evidence-of-someone-being-killed-by-a-falling-meteorite.

69 On May 1, 1860...beating: "Some Interesting Meteorite Falls of the Last Two Centuries," *International Comet Quarterly*, www.icq.eps.harvard.edu/meteorites-1.html.

69 Blowing up an asteroid—with nukes: Andrew Masterson, "Can We Nuke an Incoming Asteroid?," *Cosmos*, March 5, 2019, https://cosmosmagazine.com/space/think-we-can-nuke-away-an-incoming-asteroid-think-again.

69 Also, in 1967...Treaty: "The Outer Space Treaty Has Been Remarkably Successful—but Is It Fit for the Modern Age?," *The Conversation*, January 27, 2017, https://theconversation.com/the-outer-space-treaty-has-been-remarkably-successful-but-is-it-fit-for-the-modern-age-71381.

69 forbids the use of nuclear weapons: Outer Space Treaty, www.unoosa.org/oosa/en/ourwork/spacelaw/treaties/introouterspacetreaty.html.

69 Instead of blowing...trick: Will Lockett, "Can a Nuclear Bomb Save Us from an Asteroid?," Medium, July 19, 2020, https://medium.com/predict/can-a-nuclear-bomb-save-us-from-an-asteroid-5c77a0943503.

69 Similarly, we could push...wind: Gregory L. Matloff, "Deflecting Asteroids," *IEEE Spectrum*, March 28, 2012, https://spectrum.ieee.org/aerospace/space-flight/deflecting-asteroids.

69 Another fun idea involves paint: "Asteroids No Match for Paint Gun, Says Professor," Phys.org, February 22, 2013, https://phys.org/news/2013-02-asteroids-gun-professor.html.

70 Double Asteroid Redirection Test (DART) spacecraft: "Mission Overview," DART: Double Asteroid Redirection Test, https://dart.jhuapl.edu/Mission/index.php.

71 Near-Earth object (NEO): NASA, "Planetary Defense: Overview," updated March 14, 2019, www.nasa.gov/planetarydefense/overview.

71 99 percent of NEOs are NEAs: NASA, "Discovery Statistics," https://cneos.jpl.nasa.gov/stats/totals.html.

71 Potentially hazardous object (PHO): NASA, "Planetary Defense: Did You Know...," updated October 30, 2019, www.nasa.gov/planetarydefense/did-you-know.

CHAPTER 7

72 In April 1815, Mount Tambora: *Encyclopedia Britannica*, "Mount Tambora," updated May 27, 2020, www.britannica.com/place/Mount-Tambora.

73 In New England...lice: Doyle Rice, "200 Years Ago, We Endured a 'Year without a Summer,'" *USA Today*, June 9, 2016, www.usatoday.com/story/weather/2016/05/26/year-without-a-summer-1816-mount-tambora/84855694.

73   Mary Shelley wrote...vacation: Bryan Walsh, *End Times: A Brief Guide to the End of the World: Asteroids, Super Volcanoes, Rogue Robots, and More* (Seven Dials, 2019), pages 71–72.

73   Volcanoes are ranked...lasts: "Volcanic Explosivity Index (VEI)," Exploring the Environment, ete.cet.edu/gcc/?/volcanoes_explosivity.

74   Supervolcanoes are an eight...VEI-8 volcano: Mike Poland, "A Personal Commentary: Why I Dislike the Term 'Supervolcano' (and What We Should Be Saying Instead)," United States Geological Survey (USGS), October 7, 2019, www.usgs.gov/center-news/a-personal-commentary-why-i-dislike-term -supervolcano-and-what-we-should-be-saying.

74   In 1872, Yellowstone...park: National Park Service, "Birth of a National Park," updated February 5, 2020, www.nps.gov/yell/learn/historyculture/yellow stoneestablishment.htm.

74   Yellowstone Caldera...Yellowstone Lake: *Encyclopedia Britannica*, "Yellowstone Caldera," updated February 16, 2018, www.britannica.com/place/Yellowstone -Caldera.

74   In the past 2.1 million...ones: *Encyclopedia Britannica*, "Yellowstone Caldera."

74   Yellowstone sits on two large chambers: "Scientists Discover Massive New Magma Chamber Under Yellowstone," *NPR*, April 24, 2015, www .npr.org/sections/thetwo-way/2015/04/24/402032765/scientists-discover -massive-new-magma-chamber-under-yellowstone.

75   Yellowstone, USA: Maya Wei-Haas, "How Dangerous Are Supervolcanoes? Get the Facts," *National Geographic*, March 19, 2019, www.nationalgeographic.com /science/article/supervolcano-yellowstone.

75   Mount Vesuvius, Italy: Carly Cassella, "The World's 10 Most Devastating Volcanic Eruptions," *Australian Geographic*, January 19, 2017, www .australiangeographic.com.au/topics/science-environment/2017/01/the -worlds-10-most-devastating-volcanic-eruptions.

75   Ilopango, El Salvador: Cassella, "World's 10 Most Devastating."

75   Laki, Iceland: Cassella, "World's 10 Most Devastating."

75   Krakatoa, Indonesia: Cassella, "World's 10 Most Devastating."

75   Mount Pelée, Caribbean: Cassella, "World's 10 Most Devastating."

75   Mount Saint Helens, Washington State: National Oceanic and Atmospheric Administration (NOAA), "Mount St. Helens, Washington USA," www.ngdc .noaa.gov/hazard/stratoguide/helenfact.html.

76   In 2017, several...way: Walsh, *End Times*, page 75.

77   Lava flow will...three eruptions: Becky Oskin, "What Would Happen If Yellowstone's Supervolcano Erupted?," *Live Science*, May 2, 2016, www.livescience .com/20714-yellowstone-supervolcano-eruption.html.

77   Huge volcanoes...*nuée ardente*: USGS, "Pyroclastic Flows at Yellowstone," www.usgs.gov/volcanoes/yellowstone/pyroclastic-flows-yellowstone.

77   Scientists call it pyroclastic flow...reach 1,300°F: Robin George Andrews, "Volcanic 'Avalanches' Glide on Air, Boosting Their Deadly Speed," *National Geographic*, April 8, 2019, www.nationalgeographic.com/science/article/volcanic-avalanches-pyroclastic-flows-glide-on-air-boosting-deadly-speed.

78   ashfall will be a major issue: Walsh, *End Times*, page 77–78.

78   Temperatures will plummet...droughts: Walsh, *End Times*, page 79.

78   New York City, Washington, DC...an inch: Oskin, "What Would Happen."

79   wastewater will destroy the equipment: Walsh, *End Times*, page 77.

79   This cold spell...decade: Rice, "200 Years Ago."

80   Okmok volcano eruption in Alaska: Paul Voosen, "Alaskan Megaeruption May Have Helped End the Roman Republic," *Science*, June 22, 2020, www.sciencemag.org/news/2020/06/alaskan-mega-eruption-may-have-helped-end-roman-republic.

80   NASA's planetary defense budget: Bryan Walsh, "A Giant Volcano Could End Human Life on Earth as We Know It," *New York Times*, August 21, 2019, www.nytimes.com/2019/08/21/opinion/supervolcano-yellowstone.html.

80   The volcano hazard program: Casey Dreier, "How NASA's Planetary Defense Budget Grew by More Than 4000% in 10 Years," Planetary Society, September 26, 2019, www.planetary.org/articles/nasas-planetary-defense-budget-growth.

81   drilling down to the magma chamber: Brian H. Wilcox, Karl L. Mitchell, Florian M. Schwandner, and Rosaly M. Lopes, "Defending Human Civilization from Supervolcanic Eruptions" (2015), California Institute of Technology, https://scienceandtechnology.jpl.nasa.gov/sites/default/files/documents/DefendingCivilizationFromSupervolcanos20151015.pdf.

82   one in 730,000: Walsh, "Giant Volcano."

82   In the past 10,000...VEI 7s: Hobart M. King, "Volcanic Explosivity Index (VEI)," Geology.com, https://geology.com/stories/13/volcanic-explosivity-index.

CHAPTER 8

84   Neolithic farmers from 4,900 years ago: Ewen Callaway, "Plague Linked to the Mysterious Decline of Europe's First Farmers," *Nature News*, December 6, 2018, www.nature.com/articles/d41586-018-07673-7.

84   Black Death (1347–1351): *Encyclopedia Britannica*, "Black Death," updated November 9, 2020, www.britannica.com/event/Black-Death.

84   wiped out 60 percent of the European population: Ole Benedictow, "The Black Death: The Greatest Catastrophe Ever," *History Today*, March 2005, www.historytoday.com/archive/black-death-greatest-catastrophe-ever.

84   We now know that the plague...and die: Bob Berman, *Earth-Shattering: Violent Supernovas, Galactic Explosions, Biological Mayhem, Nuclear Meltdowns, and Other Hazards to Life in Our Universe* (Little, Brown, 2019), page 162.

84   About three days after...mammals: Benedictow, "Black Death."

84   The black rat...people: Berman, *Earth-Shattering*, pages 162–63.

85   Isaac Newton left...population died: Gillian Brockell, "During a Pandemic, Isaac Newton Had to Work from Home, Too. He Used the Time Wisely," *Washington Post*, March 12, 2020, www.washingtonpost.com/history/2020/03/12 /during-pandemic-isaac-newton-had-work-from-home-too-he-used-time-wisely.

85   Once a bacterium-carrying...possibly death: *Encyclopedia Britannica*, "Plague," updated August 6, 2020, www.britannica.com/science/plague.

86   30 to 60 percent: World Health Organization (WHO), "Plague," October 31, 2017, www.who.int/news-room/fact-sheets/detail/plague.

86   A writer in Florence...lasagna: Berman, *Earth-Shattering*, page 162.

87   medical experts thought...plague: Karin Lehnardt, "42 Catastrophic Black Death Facts," Fact Retriever, September 1, 2019, www.factretriever.com/black -death-facts.

87   1894 that the bacterium was discovered: *Encyclopedia Britannica*, "Plague."

87   This was during...worldwide: Jenny Howard, "Plague Was One of History's Deadliest Diseases—Then We Found a Cure," *National Geographic*, July 6, 2020, www.nationalgeographic.com/science/article/the-plague.

87   Bacteria have called...years: *Encyclopedia Britannica*, "Bacteria: Evolution of Bacteria," updated December 4, 2020, www.britannica.com/science/bacteria /Evolution-of-bacteria.

87   In your body...pathogen: National Human Genome Research Institute, "Bacteria," www.genome.gov/genetics-glossary/Bacteria.

88   The Egyptian pharaoh...pockmarks: "Smallpox," *National Geographic*, www .nationalgeographic.com/science/article/smallpox.

88   An infection starts...immunity: *Encyclopedia Britannica*, "Smallpox," updated July 24, 2020, www.britannica.com/science/smallpox.

88   Over 3 million Aztecs...from it: "Smallpox," *National Geographic*.

88   Smallpox spread among Native American tribes: Adrija Roychowdhury, "How Smallpox Cleared the Way for European Occupation of the Americas," *Indian Express*, May 20, 2020, https://indianexpress.com/article/research/coronavirus -how-smallpox-cleared-the-way-for-european-occupation-of-the-americas -6416791.

88   First Nations in Canada: Christopher J. Rutty, "A Pox on Our Nation," *Canada's History*, April 7, 2020, www.canadashistory.ca/explore/science-technology /a-pox-on-our-nation.

89   In the 1700s...the globe: "Smallpox," *National Geographic*.

89   And in some parts...nose: "Smallpox," *National Geographic*.

89   Or another method...person's cut: Stefan Riedel, "Edward Jenner and the History of Smallpox and Vaccination," *Baylor University Medical Center Proceedings* 18, no. 1 (January 2005): 21–25, www.ncbi.nlm.nih.gov/pmc/articles /PMC1200696.

89   2 to 3 percent of people died: Riedel, "Edward Jenner."

89   A doctor named Edward Jenner: British Society for Immunology, "Horn of Blossom the Cow (1796)," www.immunology.org/horn-blossom-the-cow-1796.

90   went on to vaccinate his infant son: "History: Edward Jenner (1749–1823)," *BBC*, www.bbc.co.uk/history/historic_figures/jenner_edward.shtml.

90   In 1934, smallpox…announced victory: *Encyclopedia Britannica*, "Smallpox."

91   Dr. Jenner did buy…funeral: Kiona N. Smith, "Why Edward Jenner Infected His Gardener's Son with Smallpox," *Forbes*, May 17, 2019, www .forbes.com/sites/kionasmith/2019/05/17/why-edward-jenner-infected-his -gardeners-son-with-smallpox.

91   COVID-19 is the illness…a pandemic: *Encyclopedia Britannica*, "Coronavirus," updated February 23, 2021, www.britannica.com/science/coronavirus -virus-group.

92   As of mid-2021…Americans: "COVID-19 Dashboard," Coronavirus Resource Center, Johns Hopkins University, accessed May 10, 2021, https://coronavirus .jhu.edu/map.html.

92   In January 2021, over 3,000 Americans: Centers for Disease Control and Prevention (CDC), "COVID Data Tracker," https://covid.cdc.gov /covid-data-tracker/#trends_dailytrendscases.

92   vaccines were approved…same time: United States Food and Drug Administration (FDA), "Pfizer-BioNTech COVID-19 Vaccine," www.fda.gov/emergency -preparedness-and-response/coronavirus-disease-2019-covid-19/pfizer -biontech-covid-19-vaccine.

93   Numbers from March 11, 2021: Don Rauf, "Coronavirus Alert: President Signs Relief Bill, Pfizer Vaccine Blocks Asymptomatic Infections, Unemployment Eases, Thursday Officially Marks One Year of Pandemic," Everyday Health, March 11, 2021, www.everydayhealth.com/coronavirus /coronavirus-alert/2021march11.

93   Americans make up only…population: "United States Population," Worldometer, www.worldometers.info/world-population/us-population.

94   12,000 to 61,000 flu deaths: CDC, "Disease Burden of Influenza," updated October 5, 2020, www.cdc.gov/flu/about/burden/index.html.

94   Ebola (Virus): *Encyclopedia Britannica*, "Ebola," updated April 1, 2021, www .britannica.com/science/Ebola.

94   The 2014–2016 Ebola epidemic: CDC, "2014–2016 Ebola Outbreak in West Africa," updated March 8, 2019, www.cdc.gov/vhf/ebola/history/2014-2016 -outbreak/index.html

94   Malaria (Parasite): *Encyclopedia Britannica*, "Malaria," updated October 2, 2020, www.britannica.com/science/malaria.

95   In 1928, scientist…the mold: *Encyclopedia Britannica*, "Alexander Fleming," updated March 27, 2021, www.britannica.com/biography/Alexander-Fleming.

95   An injectable form…World War II: *Encyclopedia Britannica*, "Penicillin," updated May 28, 2020, www.britannica.com/science/penicillin.

95   Life expectancy…in 2016: CDC, "Life Expectancy at Birth, at Age 65, and at Age 75, by Sex, Race, and Hispanic Origin: United States, Selected Years 1900–2016" (2017), www.cdc.gov/nchs/data/hus/2017/015.pdf.

95   partly thanks to the golden age of antibiotics: W. A. Adedeji, "The Treasure Called Antibiotics," *Annals of Ibadan Postgraduate Medicine* 14, no. 2 (December 2016): 56–57, www.ncbi.nlm.nih.gov/pmc/articles/PMC5354621.

95   the US sees over…American deaths: CDC, "Antibiotic Resistance Threats in the United States" (December 2019), www.cdc.gov/drugresistance/pdf/threats-report/2019-ar-threats-report-508.pdf.

96   In 2019, the Centers for Disease…all antibiotics: CDC, "Biggest Threats and Data," updated March 2, 2021, www.cdc.gov/drugresistance/biggest-threats.html.

CHAPTER 9

97   In 1500, right around…2025: Matt Rosenberg, "Current World Population and Future Projections," ThoughtCo, February 18, 2020, www.thoughtco.com/current-world-population-1435270.

97   plenty of land—about 57 million square miles: CIA, "The World Factbook," updated June 9, 2021, www.cia.gov/the-world-factbook/countries/world.

99   Art: More than a third of our crops are used for feeding livestock: Emma Bryce, "We Can Feed the World—If We Reclaim Our Crops from Livestock," *Anthropocene*, July 27, 2018, www.anthropocenemagazine.org/2018/07/we-can-feed-the-world-if-we-reclaim-our-crops-from-livestock.

99   About 50 percent of Earth's…livestock: Hannah Ritchie and Max Roser, "Land Use," Our World in Data, September 2019, https://ourworldindata.org/land-use.

99   the average American consumes a whopping 222 pounds: Megan Durisin and Shruti Date Singh, "Americans' Meat Consumption Set to Hit a Record in 2018," *Seattle Times*, January 2, 2018, www.seattletimes.com/business/americans-meat-consumption-set-to-hit-a-record-in-2018.

99   2.67 acres of land: Kristen Satre Meyer, "Which Diet Makes Best Use of Farmland? You Might Be Surprised," *Ensia*, July 22, 2016, https://ensia.com/notable/which-diet-makes-best-use-of-farmland-you-might-be-surprised.

100   Art: One pound of meat requires 260 square feet of farmland: Chelsea Harvey, "We Are Killing the Environment One Hamburger at a Time," *Business Insider*, March 5, 2015, www.businessinsider.com/one-hamburger-environment-resources-2015-2.

101   Art: seventy percent of our clean water goes to agriculture: Tariq Khokhar, "Chart: Globally, 70% of Freshwater Is Used for Agriculture," World Bank Blogs, March 22, 2017, https://blogs.worldbank.org/opendata/chart-globally-70-freshwater-used-agriculture.

101   2.1 billion people who do not have safe drinking water at home: Hannah Ritchie and Max Roser, "Clean Water," Our World in Data, November 2019, https://ourworldindata.org/water-access.

101   Mexico City, which is home to more than 21 million people: "Mexico City, Mexico Metro Area Population 1950–2021," MacroTrends, www.macrotrends.net/cities/21853/mexico-city/population.

101   Mexico City gets half...throughout the city: Christine Murray, "As Reservoirs Run Low, Mexico City Seeks Durable Fix for Water Woes," *Reuters*, December 28, 2020, www.reuters.com/article/us-mexico-water-climatechange-feature-tr/as-reservoirs-run-low-mexico-city-seeks-durable-fix-for-water-woes-idUSKBN2921BM.

102   10 to 17 percent less natural water: Murray, "As Reservoirs Run Low."

102   For decades, the city...money-saving idea: Dustin Renwick, "Five Years On, the Flint Water Crisis Is Nowhere Near Over," *National Geographic*, April 25, 2019, www.nationalgeographic.com/environment/article/flint-water-crisis-fifth-anniversary-flint-river-pollution.

102   But soon after the city...water safe: Melissa Denchak, "Flint Water Crisis: Everything You Need to Know," Natural Resources Defense Council, November 8, 2018, www.nrdc.org/stories/flint-water-crisis-everything-you-need-know.

102   The Flint River did not have...Flint's H_2O: Renwick, "Five Years On."

103   average adult man needs to drink: Mayo Clinic, "Water: How Much Should You Drink Every Day?," October 14, 2020, www.mayoclinic.org/healthy-lifestyle/nutrition-and-healthy-eating/in-depth/water/art-20044256.

103   In the US, a single person can use about 100 gallons per day: Stephen Leahy, "From Not Enough to Too Much, the World's Water Crisis Explained," *National Geographic*, March 22, 2018, www.nationalgeographic.com/science/article/world-water-day-water-crisis-explained.

103   The World Health Organization...water per day: United Nations, "The Human Right to Water and Sanitation," www.un.org/waterforlifedecade/pdf/human_right_to_water_and_sanitation_media_brief.pdf.

103   When Cape Town...thirteen gallons per day: Leahy, "From Not Enough."

103   In Mexico City, residents...per day: David Adler, "The War for Mexico's Water," *Foreign Policy*, July 31, 2015, https://foreignpolicy.com/2015/07/31/the-war-for-privatization-mexicos-water.

103   The United Nations (UN) predicts...9.7 billion: United Nations, "Growing at a Slower Pace, World Population Is Expected to Reach 9.7 Billion in 2050 and Could Peak at Nearly 11 Billion Around 2100," July 17, 2019, www.un.org/development/desa/en/news/population/world-population-prospects-2019.html.

103   Europe's and North America's...drop: United Nations, *World Population Prospects 2019*, https://population.un.org/wpp/Publications/Files/WPP2019_Highlights.pdf, page 8.

103   Asia's populations...sub-Saharan Africa's will boom: United Nations, *World Population Prospects 2019*, page 6.

104   In 1854...most of the community: Theodore H. Tulchinsky, "John Snow, Cholera, the Broad Street Pump; Waterborne Diseases Then and Now," *Case Studies in Public Health* (2018): 77–99, www.ncbi.nlm.nih.gov/pmc/articles/PMC7150208.

104   A typhus outbreak hit Los Angeles: Soumya Karlamangla, "Long before City Hall Rats, L.A. Has Struggled with the Rise of Typhus," *Los Angeles Times*, February 17, 2019, www.latimes.com/local/california/la-me-ln-typhus-20190217 -story.html.

104   The bacteria-driven disease..."camp fever": *Encyclopedia Britannica*, "Typhus," updated March 5, 2021, www.britannica.com/science/typhus.

104   Typhus thrives...homeless community: Karlamangla, "Long before City Hall Rats."

105   currently consuming the resources of 1.7 Earths: Earth Overshoot Day, "How Many Earths? How Many Countries?," www.overshootday.org/how-many -earths-or-countries-do-we-need.

105   in 2019, we emptied...July 29: Global Footprint Network, "Earth Overshoot Day 2019 Is July 29th, the Earliest Ever," June 26, 2019, www.footprintnetwork .org/2019/06/26/press-release-june-2019-earth-overshoot-day.

105   Earth Overshoot Day—was August 22: Earth Overshoot Day, "How the Date of Earth Overshoot Day 2020 Was Calculated," August 25, 2020, www.overshootday .org/2020-calculation.

106   if the rest of the world...five Earths: Earth Overshoot Day, "How Many Earths?"

106   gross national income per capita: *Encyclopedia Britannica*, "Gross National Income," updated February 4, 2020, www.britannica.com/topic/gross-national -income.

106   For the United States...$11,571: World Bank, "GNI per Capita, Atlas Method (Current US$)," https://data.worldbank.org/indicator/NY.GNP.PCAP.CD.

106   America has the highest...nations: Grant Suneson, "These Are the 25 Richest Countries in the World," *USA Today*, July 7, 2019, www.usatoday.com/story /money/2019/07/07/richest-countries-in-the-world/39630693.

106   The fifty richest...US citizens: Ben Steverman and Alexandre Tanzi, "The 50 Richest Americans Are Worth as Much as the Poorest 165 Million," *Bloomberg*, October 8, 2020, www.bloomberg.com/news/articles/2020-10-08 /top-50-richest-people-in-the-us-are-worth-as-much-as-poorest-165-million.

106   Over 1.3 million...of students: Ariella Meltzer, Diana Quintero, and Jon Valant, "Better Serving the Needs of America's Homeless Students," Brookings Institution, October 24, 2019, www.brookings.edu/blog/brown-center -chalkboard/2019/10/24/better-serving-the-needs-of-americas-homeless -students.

106   Approximately 13 million...kids: Feeding America, "One Year Later Feeding America Asks America 'How Many Facing Hunger Is Too Many?,'" March 9, 2021, www.feedingamerica.org/about-us/press-room/one-year-later.

107   "It might be doubted...ceased to exist": Thomas Jefferson to Francis van der Kemp, quoted in "Species Extinction," Thomas Jefferson Foundation, www .monticello.org/site/research-and-collections/species-extinction.

107   trace the demise of megafauna...globe: Yuval Noah Harari, *Sapiens: A Brief History of Humankind* (Harper Perennial, 2018), page 72.

107   mammoths lived on...Antarctica: *Encyclopedia Britannica*, "Mammoth," updated February 26, 2021, www.britannica.com/animal/mammoth-extinct-mammal.

108   In 1796, this bird...crop failure: Lenore Newman, *Lost Feast: Culinary Extinction and the Future of Food* (ECW Press, 2019), page 104.

108   numbered in the billions: *Encyclopedia Britannica*, "Passenger Pigeon," updated June 13, 2019, www.britannica.com/animal/passenger-pigeon.

108   made up 40 percent of the total bird population, Newman, *Lost Feast*, page 101.

108   In 1833, John James Audubon...for days: David Biello, "3 Billion to Zero: What Happened to the Passenger Pigeon?," *Scientific American*, June 27, 2014, www.scientificamerican.com/article/3-billion-to-zero-what-happened-to-the-passenger-pigeon.

108   birds' dung falling like melting snow: John James Audubon, *Ornithological Biography, Volume 1*, 1832. www.audubon.org/birds-of-america/passenger-pigeon.

108   A single gunshot...mid-1890s: Newman, *Lost Feast*, pages 99–114.

109   Martha, the last of her species: Smithsonian National Museum of Natural History, "Martha, the Last Passenger Pigeon," https://naturalhistory.si.edu/research/vertebrate-zoology/birds/collections-overview/martha-last-passenger-pigeon.

CHAPTER 10

111   Our first battle...Middle East: Jonathan Strickland, "When and Why Did We Invent War?," HowStuffWorks, August 30, 2010, https://science.howstuffworks.com/invent-war.htm.

112   In 1939, German scientists discovered fission: United States Department of Energy, "Manhattan Project: Early Government Support (1939–1942)," www.osti.gov/opennet/manhattan-project-history/Events/1939-1942/1939-1942.htm.

112   Albert Einstein...Committee on Uranium: Atomic Heritage Foundation, "The Einstein-Szilard Letter—1939," July 18, 2017, www.atomicheritage.org/history/einstein-szilard-letter-1939.

112   In February 1940...code name the Manhattan Project: *Encyclopedia Britannica*, "Manhattan Project," updated September 10, 2020, www.britannica.com/event/Manhattan-Project.

112   Thousands of Americans...a war effort: Erin Blakemore, "WWII's Atomic Bomb Program Was So Secretive That Even Many of the Participants Were in the Dark," *Washington Post*, November 2, 2019, www.washingtonpost.com/science/wwiis-atomic-bomb-program-was-so-secretive-that-even-many-of-the-participants-were-in-the-dark/2019/10/31/8d92d16c-fb7e-11e9-8906-ab6b60de9124_story.html.

112   Even in Congress...ultimate goal: Peter Pry, *The Role of Congress in the Strategic Posture of the United States, 1942–1960: Manhattan Project to the New Look* (United States Defense Threat Reduction Agency, May 2010), https://www.hsdl.org/?abstract&did=715948.

112   Einstein never worked...pacifist: American Museum of Natural History, "The Manhattan Project," www.amnh.org/exhibitions/einstein/peace-and-war/the-manhattan-project.

113   Fission—Atoms Splitting Apart: United States Department of Energy, "Fission and Fusion: What Is the Difference?," April 1, 2021, www.energy.gov/ne/articles/fission-and-fusion-what-difference.

113   Weapons that use fission...atomic bombs: *Encyclopedia Britannica*, "Atomic Bomb," updated August 27, 2020, www.britannica.com/technology/atomic-bomb.

113   Fusion—Atoms Coming Together: United States Department of Energy, "Fission and Fusion."

113   Weapons that use fusion...hydrogen bombs: *Encyclopedia Britannica*, "Thermonuclear Bomb," updated January 28, 2020, www.britannica.com/technology/thermonuclear-bomb.

114   The first test...middle of the desert: *Encyclopedia Britannica*, "Trinity," www.britannica.com/topic/Trinity-atomic-bomb-test.

114   Because of their uncertainty...ten tons of TNT: Bryan Walsh, *End Times: A Brief Guide to the End of the World: Asteroids, Super Volcanoes, Rogue Robots, and More* (Seven Dials, 2019), page 90.

114   Trinity achieved...destructiveness: *Encyclopedia Britannica*, "Nuclear Weapon: Racing to Build the Bombs," updated December 12, 2019, www.britannica.com/technology/nuclear-weapon/Racing-to-build-the-bombs.

114   On August 6, 1945...months after the bombings: *Encyclopedia Britannica*, "World War II: Hiroshima and Nagasaki," updated May 15, 2021, www.britannica.com/event/World-War-II/Hiroshima-and-Nagasaki.

115   On August 15, a radio...September 2: United States Department of Energy, "Manhattan Project: Japan Surrenders (August 10–15, 1945)," www.osti.gov/opennet/manhattan-project-history/Events/1945/surrender.htm.

115   At this point in World War II...including children: National Park Service, "Harry S Truman's Decision to Use the Atomic Bomb," updated October 25, 2017, www.nps.gov/articles/trumanatomicbomb.htm.

115   Another theory speculates...expensive: Walter Pincus, "Truman Didn't Hesitate to Drop Atomic Bomb on Japan," *Washington Post*, July 16, 1995, www.washingtonpost.com/archive/politics/1995/07/16/truman-didnt-hesitate-to-drop-atomic-bomb-on-japan/0093ae4e-a935-421c-9da3-b6048cc7a6a5.

115   he didn't even know...oath of office: Atomic Heritage Foundation, "Harry Truman," www.atomicheritage.org/profile/harry-truman.

116   Trinity test in July...100,000 civilians: *Encyclopedia Britannica*, "The Decision to Use the Atomic Bomb," updated August 5, 2010, www.britannica.com/topic/Trumans-decision-to-use-the-bomb-712569.

116   discussion of just showing off America's nuclear bomb: National Park Service, "Harry S Truman's Decision."

116   The site of Hiroshima...committee meetings: Atomic Heritage Foundation, "Target Committee Recommendations," www.atomicheritage.org/key-documents/target-committee-recommendations.

116   Prior to August 6, 1945...destroy a city: *Encyclopedia Britannica*, "Know about the Catastrophic Impact of the Atomic Bombing of Hiroshima, Japan, during World War II," www.britannica.com/video/219022/infographic-explained-atomic-bombing-Hiroshima.

117   The three-hour firebombing of Tokyo: Brad Lendon and Emiko Jozuka, "History's Deadliest Air Raid Happened in Tokyo during World War II and You've Probably Never Heard of It," *CNN*, March 8, 2020, www.cnn.com/2020/03/07/asia/japan-tokyo-fire-raids-operation-meetinghouse-intl-hnk/index.html.

118   The bomb ignited 1,900 feet: *Encyclopedia Britannica*, "Racing to Build."

119   The descriptions of the aftermath of the atomic bombs are from Ishaan Tharoor, "What It Was Like to Survive the Atomic Bombing of Hiroshima," *Washington Post*, May 27, 2016, www.washingtonpost.com/news/worldviews/wp/2015/08/05/what-it-was-like-to-survive-the-atomic-bombing-of-hiroshima/; and Lily Rothman, "After the Bomb: Survivors of the Atomic Blasts in Hiroshima and Nagasaki Share Their Stories," *Time*, https://time.com/after-the-bomb.

120   By 1960...big bombs: United States Department of Energy, "Manhattan Project: Nuclear Proliferation (1949–Present)," www.osti.gov/opennet/manhattan-project-history/Events/1945-present/proliferation.htm.

120   Tsar Bomba—also known as Big Ivan: *Encyclopedia Britannica*, "Tsar Bomba," updated October 23, 2020, www.britannica.com/topic/Tsar-Bomba.

120   biggest *T. rex* ever found: Michael Greshko, "World's Biggest T. Rex Discovered," *National Geographic*, March 26, 2019, www.nationalgeographic.com/science/article/worlds-biggest-t-rex-found-in-canada-scotty-dinosaur.

121   70,000 nuclear warheads were stockpiled worldwide: Hans M. Kristensen and Matt Korda, "Status of World Nuclear Forces," Federation of American Scientists, updated May 2021, https://fas.org/issues/nuclear-weapons/status-world-nuclear-forces.

121   to 13,100, thanks to treaties and global agreements: Kristensen and Korda, "Status of World Nuclear Forces."

121   over 3 billion people live in rural areas: Hannah Ritchie and Max Roser, "Urbanization," Our World in Data, November 2019, https://ourworldindata.org/urbanization.

122   "The ability to live...commodity": Rothman, "After the Bomb."

CHAPTER 11

123   Our sun is a G2 V...another star dying: *Encyclopedia Britannica*, "Sun," updated February 4, 2021, www.britannica.com/place/Sun.

123   last a total of around 10 billion years: *Encyclopedia Britannica*, "Sun: Evolution of the Sun," updated February 4, 2021, www.britannica.com/place/Sun /Evolution.

124   the temperature is about 10,000°F…99.8 percent: National Aeronautics and Space Administration (NASA), "Our Sun," updated December 19, 2019, https:// solarsystem.nasa.gov/solar-system/sun/in-depth.

124   its surface moves at…solar maximum: NASA, "Our Sun."

124   The next solar maximum…summer of 2025: National Oceanic and Atmospheric Administration (NOAA), "Hello Solar Cycle 25," September 15, 2020, www.weather .gov/news/201509-solar-cycle.

124   There's enough hydrogen…3.5 billion more years: Jillian Scudder, "The Sun Won't Die for 5 Billion Years, so Why Do Humans Have Only 1 Billion Years Left on Earth?," Phys.org, February 13, 2015, https://phys.org/news/2015-02 -sun-wont-die-billion-years.html.

125   Between 1645 and 1715: Bob Berman, *Earth-Shattering: Violent Supernovas, Galactic Explosions, Biological Mayhem, Nuclear Meltdowns, and Other Hazards to Life in Our Universe* (Little, Brown, 2019), page 278.

125   The Thames in London froze: *Encyclopedia Britannica*, "Maunder Minimum," updated October 16, 2016, www.britannica.com/science/Maunder-minimum.

125   Glaciers moved over farmland in Norway: *Encyclopedia Britannica*, "Maunder Minimum."

125   In 1 billion years, the sun will be: Berman, *Earth-Shattering*, pages 278–79.

126   when it runs out of hydrogen: Eric Betz, "Here's What Happens to the Solar System When the Sun Dies," *Discover Magazine*, February 6, 2020, www.discover magazine.com/the-sciences/heres-what-happens-to-the-solar-system-when -the-sun-dies.

128   Our sun will not maintain…become a white dwarf: Ethan Siegel, "This Is What Will Happen to Our Sun after It Dies," *Forbes*, June 11, 2019, www.forbes.com /sites/startswithabang/2019/06/11/this-is-what-will-happen-to-our-sun-after -it-dies.

128   A teaspoon of a white dwarf: Robert Naeye, "One Weird Type of Star Acts Like Another," NASA, January 2, 2008, www.nasa.gov/topics/universe/features /whitedwarf_pulsar.html.

128   This ultra-hot star will cool down…supernova: Siegel, "This Is What Will Happen."

128   The sun will still be the size of Earth: John Wenz, "Four Types of Stars That Will Not Exist for Billions or Even Trillions of Years," *Smithsonian Magazine*, January 18, 2019, www.smithsonianmag.com/science-nature/four-types-stars -will-not-exist-billions-or-even-trillions-years-180971299.

129   as many as 300 million…sun-like stars: SETI Institute, "How Many Habitable Planets Are Out There?," October 29, 2020, www.seti.org/press-release /how-many-habitable-planets-are-out-there.

129 different from solar flares, but they can occur: Max Gleber, "The Difference between Flares and CMEs," NASA, August 7, 2017, www.nasa.gov/content /goddard/the-difference-between-flares-and-cmes.

129 A *Scientific American*...hurricanes: Sten F. Odenwald and James L. Green, "Bracing the Satellite Infrastructure for a Solar Superstorm," *Scientific American*, August 1, 2008, www.scientificamerican.com/article/bracing-for-a-solar -superstorm.

129 flares are flashes...to Earth: Gleber, "Difference between Flares and CMEs."

129 CMEs are clouds...plasma: Calla Cofield, "Mysteriously Powerful Particles from Solar Explosions Unveiled in New Study," *Scientific American*, February 2, 2016, www.scientificamerican.com/article/mysteriously-powerful-particles -from-solar-explosions-unveiled-in-new-study.

129 fifteen hours to several days: NOAA, "Coronal Mass Ejections," www.swpc .noaa.gov/phenomena/coronal-mass-ejections.

129 Our magnetic poles tug...southern lights: Gleber, "Difference between Flares and CMEs."

129 And our atmosphere also...the surface: Deborah Byrd, "Are Solar Storms Dangerous to Us?," *EarthSky*, January 30, 2020, https://earthsky.org/space /are-solar-storms-dangerous-to-us.

130 In the late summer of 1859: Odenwald and Green, "Bracing the Satellite."

130 A solar storm this size...continent: Odenwald and Green, "Bracing the Satellite."

131 called a 500-year event: Odenwald and Green, "Bracing the Satellite."

131 the second CME...seventeen hours: Odenwald and Green, "Bracing the Satellite."

131 the Deep Space Climate...storm's arrival: NOAA, "NOAA Satellite and Infor- mation Service Deep Space Climate Observatory (DSCOVR)," www.nesdis .noaa.gov/sites/default/files/asset/document/dscovr_program_overview _info_sheet.pdf.

CHAPTER 12

133 The name is a mistake...*new stars*: Andy Briggs, "What Is a Supernova?" *EarthSky*, November 12, 2020, https://earthsky.org/astronomy-essentials/definition-what-is -a-supernova.

133 half of the Milky Way's solar systems are multi-star: *Encyclopedia Britannica*, "Binary Star," updated September 5, 2019, www.britannica.com/science/binary -star.

134 A supernova Type Ia occurs...white dwarf explodes: Andrea Thompson, "What Is a Supernova?," Space.com, February 8, 2018, www.space.com/6638-supernova .html.

134 up to three times more luminous than a Type II: *Encyclopedia Britannica*, "Su- pernova," updated March 13, 2020, www.britannica.com/science/supernova.

134   A Type II supernova...create a neutron star: Fraser Cain, "What Are the Different Kinds of Supernovae?," Phys.org, March 15, 2016, https://phys.org /news/2016-03-kinds-supernovae.html.

135   a twelve-mile-wide...50 billion tons: *Encyclopedia Britannica*, "Supernova."

135   twenty-five times bigger than our sun: Cain, "What Are the Different Kinds."

135   Confusing side note...hydrogen: Thompson, "What Is a Supernova?"

136   the Milky Way experiences three supernovae: Rachel Courtland, "Milky Way's Youngest Supernova Found," *Nature*, May 15, 2008, www.nature.com /news/2008/080515/full/news.2008.827.html.

136   none of our closest neighbors are capable: "What's a Safe Distance between Us and a Supernova?," *EarthSky*, May 11, 2018, https://earthsky.org /astronomy-essentials/supernove-distance.

136   It was the late 1960s: Gavin Rowell, "A Collapsing Star in a Distant Galaxy Fired Out Some of the Most Energetic Gamma Rays Ever Seen," *The Conversation*, November 20, 2019, https://theconversation.com/a-collapsing-star-in -a-distant-galaxy-fired-out-some-of-the-most-energetic-gamma-rays-ever -seen-127114.

136   In a GRB, all that energy is directed...lightsaber: Adam Mann, "What Is a Gamma-Ray Burst?," Space.com, January 15, 2020, www.space.com/gamma -ray-burst.html.

136   The energy from a ten-second GRB: National Aeronautics and Space Administration (NASA), "Gamma Rays," https://science.nasa.gov/ems/12_gammarays.

137   hypernova, which is a...long GRBs: Amber Jorgenson, "Astronomers May Have Finally Connected Supernovae and Gamma Ray Bursts," *Astronomy*, January 21, 2019, https://astronomy.com/news/2019/01/astronomers-may-have-finally -connected-supernovae-and-gamma-ray-bursts.

137   last two seconds to a few hours: NASA, "Gamma-Ray Bursts," HubbleSite, updated May 31, 2019, https://hubblesite.org/contents/articles/gamma-ray-bursts.

137   GRBs can also be created...two seconds: NASA, "Gamma-Ray Bursts."

137   Short bursts are...more often: Charles Q. Choi, "Did Deadly Gamma-Ray Burst Cause a Mass Extinction on Earth?," *Live Science*, December 8, 2014, www .livescience.com/49040-gamma-ray-burst-mass-extinction.html.

137   NASA satellites catalog...the universe: Mann, "What Is a Gamma-Ray Burst?"

138   If directed squarely at Earth...nuclear explosion: Choi, "Did Deadly Gamma -Ray Burst."

138   Without our ozone layer: Susan Hunt, "What Will Happen to Life on Earth If Ozone Depletion Continues?," Ozone Depletion, September 3, 2019, www .ozonedepletion.co.uk/what-will-happen-life-earth-if-ozone-depletion -continues.html.

138   GRBs have yet to be witnessed in the Milky Way: "Doomed Star in Milky Way Threatens Rare Gamma-Ray Burst," Phys.org, November 19, 2018, https://phys .org/news/2018-11-doomed-star-milky-threatens-rare.html.

138   kicked off the Ordovician-Silurian extinction: Choi, "Did Deadly Gamma-Ray Burst."

138   The theory is a hypernova...ice age: Michele Diodati, "Gamma-Ray Bursts and Collapsing Stars," Medium, February 26, 2020, https://medium.com /amazing-science/gamma-ray-bursts-and-collapsing-stars-29ca7f206c83.

139   the Milky Way is one of hundreds of billions of galaxies: Eric Mack, "NASA Spacecraft Discovers the Universe Is Less Crowded Than We Thought," CNET, January 12, 2021, www.cnet.com/news/nasa-spacecraft-discovers-the -universe-is-less-crowded-than-we-thought.

139   astronomers have confirmed the existence of exoplanets: NASA, "What Is an Exoplanet?," updated April 2, 2021, https://exoplanets.nasa.gov/what-is-an -exoplanet/overview.

139   The first confirmed exoplanet...51 Pegasi b: Encyclopedia Britannica, "51 Pegasi b," October 10, 2019, www.britannica.com/place/51-Pegasi-b-planet.

139   estimate there are millions, maybe billions, or even trillions more: Korey Haynes, "How Many Exoplanets Have Been Discovered, and How Many Are Waiting to Be Found?," Discover Magazine, February 12, 2020, www.discover magazine.com/the-sciences/how-many-exoplanets-have-been-discovered -and-how-many-are-waiting-to-be.

139   the controversial Drake equation: Encyclopedia Britannica, "Drake Equation," updated April 26, 2020, www.britannica.com/science/Drake-equation.

141   The NASA spacecraft Voyager 1...solar system: NASA, "Voyager—Planetary Voyage," https://voyager.jpl.nasa.gov/mission/science/planetary-voyage.

141   in about 40,000 years, Voyager 1...operational: NASA, "Voyager—Interstellar Mission," https://voyager.jpl.nasa.gov/mission/interstellar-mission.

142   radio waves to communicate...visible light waves: SETI (Search for Extraterrestrial Intelligence) Institute, "SETI Observations," www.seti.org /seti-institute/project/details/seti-observations.

142   humans have been sending...cables: Adam Mann, "Want to Talk to Aliens? Try Changing the Technological Channel beyond Radio," Scientific American, September 2, 2020, www.scientificamerican.com/article /want-to-talk-to-aliens-try-changing-the-technological-channel-beyond-radio.

142   The SETI (Search for Extraterrestrial Intelligence)...aliens: SETI Institute, "SETI Observations."

PART III

CHAPTER 13

147   Climate is weather during a specific season: National Centers for Environmental Information, "What's the Difference between Weather and Climate?," updated August 7, 2020, www.ncei.noaa.gov/news/weather-vs-climate.

148   "Climate is what you expect, weather is what you get": National Oceanic and Atmospheric Administration (NOAA), "What Is the Difference between Weather and Climate?," updated February 26, 2021, https://oceanservice.noaa .gov/facts/weather_climate.html.

148   This is simply the rising of Earth's surface temperature: *Encyclopedia Britannica*, "Global Warming," updated March 16, 2021, www.britannica.com/science /global-warming.

148   a change to the climate: *Encyclopedia Britannica*, "Climate Change," updated April 27, 2021, www.britannica.com/science/climate-change.

149   Average surface temperature of Mars: *Encyclopedia Britannica*, "Mars," updated May 6, 2021, www.britannica.com/place/Mars-planet.

149   Average surface temperature of Earth in the twentieth century: Rebecca Lindsey and LuAnn Dahlman, "Climate Change: Global Temperature," NOAA, March 15, 2021, www.climate.gov/news-features/understanding-climate/climate-change -global-temperature.

149   Working or playing above this temperature could be deadly: David Wallace-Wells, *The Uninhabitable Earth: Life after Warming* (Penguin Random House, 2020), page 40.

149   Average surface temperature of Venus: *Encyclopedia Britannica*, "Venus," updated October 22, 2020, www.britannica.com/place/Venus-planet.

149   Earth's temperature rise since 1850: Intergovernmental Panel on Climate Change (IPCC), *Special Report: Global Warming of 1.5 °C*, www.ipcc.ch/sr15.

149   The temperature-rise path we are on: "Global Temperatures on Track for 3-5 Degree Rise by 2100: U.N.," *Reuters*, November 29, 2018, www.reuters.com /article/us-climate-change-un/global-temperatures-on-track-for-3-5-degree -rise-by-2100-u-n-idUSKCN1NY186.

150   These include crude oil, natural gas, and coal: Melissa Denchak, "Fossil Fuels: The Dirty Facts," Natural Resources Defense Council, January 29, 2018, www .nrdc.org/stories/fossil-fuels-dirty-facts.

150   Our planet is wrapped in a protective layer: *Encyclopedia Britannica*, "Earth: The Atmosphere of Earth," updated May 6, 2021, www.britannica.com/place /Earth/The-atmosphere.

151   Venus's heavy atmosphere…464°C: *Encyclopedia Britannica*, "Atmosphere: The Atmospheres of Other Planets," updated January 11, 2021, www.britannica .com/science/atmosphere/The-atmospheres-of-other-planets.

153   Our most common GHGs are: United States Environmental Protection Agency (EPA), "Global Greenhouse Gas Emissions Data," www.epa.gov/ghgemissions /global-greenhouse-gas-emissions-data.

155   These human activities are the biggest contributors: Hannah Ritchie and Max Roser, "Emissions by Sector," Our World in Data, August 2020, https:// ourworldindata.org/emissions-by-sector.

156   food production…25 percent of GHG emissions: Hannah Ritchie, "Food Production Is Responsible for One-Quarter of the World's Greenhouse Gas Emissions," Our World in Data, November 6, 2019, https://ourworldindata.org/food-ghg-emissions.

156   estimated that cooling…10 percent of emissions: Wallace-Wells, *Uninhabitable Earth*, page 42.

156   in 2019, the world broke…in 3 million years: Rebecca Lindsey, "Climate Change: Atmospheric Carbon Dioxide," NOAA, August 14, 2020, www.climate.gov/news-features/understanding-climate/climate-change-atmospheric-carbon-dioxide.

156   atmospheric CO_2 was approximately 280 parts per million: Lindsey, "Climate Change."

156   And since, the planet's temperature has gone up 1°C: IPCC, *Special Report*.

157   The Union…net-zero carbon emissions by 2050: Union of Concerned Scientists, "Climate Solutions," www.ucsusa.org/climate/solutions.

157   The top polluting countries: Johannes Friedrich, Mengpin Ge, and Andrew Pickens, "This Interactive Chart Shows Changes in the World's Top 10 Emitters," World Resources Institute, December 10, 2020, www.wri.org/insights/interactive-chart-shows-changes-worlds-top-10-emitters.

157   This group emits two-thirds…population: Mengpin Ge and Johannes Friedrich, "4 Charts Explain Greenhouse Gas Emissions by Countries and Sectors," World Resources Institute, February 6, 2020, www.wri.org/insights/4-charts-explain-greenhouse-gas-emissions-countries-and-sectors.

158   In 2015, representatives…climate crisis: *Encyclopedia Britannica*, "Paris Agreement," updated January 27, 2021, www.britannica.com/topic/Paris-Agreement-2015.

158   global warming should be held…than 1.5°C: Paris Agreement to the United Nations Framework Convention on Climate Change, December 12, 2015, T.I.A.S. No. 16-1104, https://treaties.un.org/doc/Treaties/2016/02/20160215%2006-03%20PM/Ch_XXVII-7-d.pdf.

158   the no-change-to-gas-emissions path…century: "Global Temperatures on Track."

158   The US aimed to cut…by 2025: U.S. Cover Note INDC and Accompanying Information, https://www4.unfccc.int/sites/submissions/INDC/Submission%20Pages/submissions.aspx.

158   Syria and Nicaragua: United Nations, "Chapter XXVII, Environment, 7. d Paris Agreement," accessed June 14, 2021, https://treaties.un.org/Pages/ViewDetails.aspx?src=IND&mtdsg_no=XXVII-7-d&chapter=27&clang=_en

159   Morocco and The Gambia…1.5°C target: Climate Action Tracker, "Countries," https://climateactiontracker.org/countries.

159   reducing greenhouse gas emissions: "The United States of America Nationally Determined Contribution," www4.unfccc.int/sites/ndcstaging/Published Documents/United%20States%20of%20America%20First/United%20States%20NDC%20April%2021%202021%20Final.pdf.

160   the United Nations came out...1.5°C of warming: IPCC, *Special Report*.

160   Current Progress (as of 2019): EPA, "Inventory of U.S. Greenhouse Gas Emissions and Sinks," www.epa.gov/ghgemissions/inventory-us-greenhouse-gas -emissions-and-sinks.

161   Ninety-seven percent of climate scientists...activities: John Cook et al., "Consensus on Consensus: A Synthesis of Consensus Estimates on Human-Caused Global Warming," *Environmental Research Letters* 11, no. 4 (April 2016), https:// iopscience.iop.org/article/10.1088/1748-9326/11/4/048002.

161   "We are more sure that greenhouse gas...cancer": Kate Marvel, quoted in Jeff Berardelli, "10 Common Myths about Climate Change—and What Science Really Says," *CBS News*, February 27, 2020, www.cbsnews.com/news /climate-change-myths-what-science-really-says.

161   Earth's temperature is rising...2,000 years: Doyle Rice, "Climate Is Warming Faster Than It Has in the Last 2,000 Years," *USA Today*, July 24, 2019, www.usa today.com/story/news/nation/2019/07/24/global-warming-climate-warming -faster-than-has-last-2-000-years/1816664001.

162   global CO_2 emissions increased between 2015 and 2018: Megan Darby, "After Five Years, Here Are Five Things the Paris Agreement Achieved—and Didn't," *Climate Home News*, September 12, 2020, www.climatechangenews.com /2020/12/09/five-years-five-things-paris-agreement-achieved-didnt/.

162   analogy from the *New York Times*: Kendra Pierre-Louis, "Why Is the Cold Weather So Extreme If the Earth Is Warming?," *New York Times*, January 31, 2019, www.nytimes.com/interactive/2019/climate/winter-cold-weather.html.

CHAPTER 14

163   pre-industrial levels: Intergovernmental Panel on Climate Change (IPCC), *Special Report: Global Warming of 1.5 °C*, www.ipcc.ch/sr15.

163   a 5°C bump by the end of the century: Jeff Tollefson, "How Hot Will Earth Get by 2100?," *Nature*, April 22, 2020, www.nature.com/articles/d41586-020-01125-x.

163   warm air can hold more moisture: National Centers for Environmental Information, "A Warming Earth Is Also a Wetter Earth," November 18, 2020, www .ncei.noaa.gov/news/warming-earth-also-wetter-earth.

164   most cars can be swept away...water: National Oceanic and Atmospheric Administration (NOAA), "Flood Safety Rules," www.weather.gov/mlb/flashflood _rules.

164   scientists don't expect *more* hurricanes: Veronica Penney, "5 Things We Know about Climate Change and Hurricanes," *New York Times*, November 10, 2020, www.nytimes.com/2020/11/10/climate/climate-change-hurricanes.html.

164   they do predict more intense hurricanes: Henry Fountain, "Climate Change Is Making Hurricanes Stronger, Researchers Find," *New York Times*, May 18, 2020, www.nytimes.com/2020/05/18/climate/climate-changes-hurricane -intensity.html.

164 Hurricanes are judged...per hour: NOAA, "Saffir-Simpson Hurricane Wind Scale," www.nhc.noaa.gov/aboutsshws.php.

165 more *frequent* thing in the northeastern United States: Chelsea Harvey, "Love Snow? Here's How It's Changing," *Scientific American*, January 28, 2019, www.scientificamerican.com/article/love-snow-heres-how-its-changing.

165 warmer air holds more water...form: Chris Mooney, "Global Warming Could Make Blizzards Worse," *Washington Post*, January 26, 2015, www.washingtonpost.com/news/energy-environment/wp/2015/01/26/global-warming-could-make-blizzards-worse.

165 Flooding has killed over 950 Americans: Statista, "Number of Lives Lost Due to Floods and Flash Floods in the U.S. from 1995 to 2019," January 15, 2021, www.statista.com/statistics/203709/number-of-fatalities-caused-by-floods-and-flash-floods-in-the-us.

165 In 2017, Hurricane Harvey...world: Michael Greshko, "Climate Change Likely Supercharged Hurricane Harvey," *National Geographic*, December 13, 2017, www.nationalgeographic.com/science/article/climate-change-study-hurricane-harvey-flood.

165 From 2008 to 2018, the northeastern...decades: "Messy Snowstorm Hits the East Coast," *New York Times*, February 14, 2021, www.nytimes.com/live/2020/12/17/nyregion/winter-storm-gail.

165 Interestingly, scientists have not found...new: Doyle Rice, "Record Cold, Intense Storms and Tornadoes amid Global Warming: Could There Be a Connection?," *USA Today*, February 23, 2021, www.usatoday.com/story/news/nation/2021/02/17/global-warming-record-cold-intense-storms-tornadoes/6780433002.

166 2°C warming means increased droughts worldwide: IPCC, *Special Report*.

166 In 2017, a man in Arizona: Andrea Diaz, "Officials Release Video from Gender Reveal Party That Ignited a 47,000-Acre Wildfire," *CNN*, November 28, 2018, www.cnn.com/2018/11/27/us/arizona-gender-reveal-party-sawmill-wildfire-trnd/index.html.

166 And in 2020, a gender-reveal event: Christina Morales and Allyson Waller, "A Gender-Reveal Celebration Is Blamed for a Wildfire. It Isn't the First Time," *New York Times*, September 18, 2020, www.nytimes.com/2020/09/07/us/gender-reveal-party-wildfire.html.

166 Wildfires in the United States...1999: Union of Concerned Scientists, "The Connection between Climate Change and Wildfires," March 11, 2020, www.ucsusa.org/resources/climate-change-and-wildfires.

166 The US fire season is seventy-eight days longer: Matt Richtel and Fernanda Santos, "Wildfires, Once Confined to a Season, Burn Earlier and Longer," *New York Times*, April 12, 2016, www.nytimes.com/2016/04/13/science/wildfires-season-global-warming.html.

166 Between 1992 and 2015, lightning...damage: John Schwartz and Veronica Penney, "In the West, Lightning Grows as a Cause of Damaging Fires," *New York Times*, October 23, 2020, www.nytimes.com/interactive/2020/10/23/climate/west-lightning-wildfires.html.

167   But in 2016, a twelve-year-old boy: "As Earth Warms, the Diseases That May Lie within Permafrost Become a Bigger Worry," *Scientific American*, November 1, 2016, www.scientificamerican.com/article/as-earth-warms-the-diseases-that-may-lie-within-permafrost-become-a-bigger-worry.

167   RNA fragments of the…plague: Jasmin Fox-Skelly, "There Are Diseases Hidden in Ice, and They Are Waking Up," *BBC*, May 4, 2017, www.bbc.com/earth/story/20170504-there-are-diseases-hidden-in-ice-and-they-are-waking-up.

168   Scientists have found 30,000-year-old viruses: "As Earth Warms."

168   Scientists have revived…glacier: Jamie Sarao, "The Climate Crisis Will Cause Once-Dormant Viruses to Reemerge," Earth.org, July 16, 2020, https://earth.org/climate-crisis-will-cause-once-dormant-viruses-to-reemerge.

168   Since the start of the twenty-first century: Michon Scott, "2020 Arctic Air Temperatures Continue a Long-Term Warming Streak," NOAA, December 8, 2020, www.climate.gov/news-features/featured-images/2020-arctic-air-temperatures-continue-long-term-warming-streak.

168   oceans absorb 90 percent of the planet's warming: Chelsea Harvey, "Oceans Are Warming Faster Than Predicted," *Scientific American*, January 11, 2019, www.scientificamerican.com/article/oceans-are-warming-faster-than-predicted.

168   They're also sucking up…acidic: NOAA, "Ocean Acidification," updated April 1, 2020, www.noaa.gov/education/resource-collections/ocean-coasts/ocean-acidification.

169   At just 1.5°C of warming…coral reefs: IPCC, *Special Report*.

169   Over half a billion people…reef ecosystems: NOAA, "Coral Reef Ecosystems," updated February 1, 2019, www.noaa.gov/education/resource-collections/marine-life/coral-reef-ecosystems.

169   Like on land, the oceans…ago: Kendra Pierre-Louis and Nadja Popovich, "Ocean Heat Waves Are Threatening Marine Life," *New York Times*, March 4, 2019, www.nytimes.com/2019/03/04/climate/marine-heat-waves.html.

170   All of Earth's ice melts: "What the World Would Look Like If All the Ice Melted," *National Geographic*, September 2013, www.nationalgeographic.com/magazine/article/rising-seas-ice-melt-new-shoreline-maps.

170   Depending on what actions humans…measurements: Rebecca Lindsey, "Climate Change: Global Sea Level," NOAA, January 25, 2021, www.climate.gov/news-features/understanding-climate/climate-change-global-sea-level.

171   Maldives and the Marshall Islands could be washed away: Jon Letman, "Rising Seas Give Island Nation a Stark Choice: Relocate or Elevate," *National Geographic*, November 19, 2018, www.nationalgeographic.com/environment/article/rising-seas-force-marshall-islands-relocate-elevate-artificial-islands.

171   Since 1880, global sea levels…the century: Lindsey, "Climate Change."

171   By 2050, over 150 million…floods: Chris Mooney, "Scientists Triple Their Estimates of the Number of People Threatened by Rising Seas," *Washington Post*, October 29, 2019, www.washingtonpost.com/climate-environment/2019/10/29/scientists-triple-their-estimates-number-people-threatened-by-rising-seas.

171   Of the ten largest cities...coastal: UN Atlas of the Oceans, "Human Settlements on the Coast," www.oceansatlas.org/subtopic/en/c/114.

171   Our upper limit is about 35°C in high humidity: David Wallace-Wells, *The Uninhabitable Earth: Life after Warming* (Penguin Random House, 2020), page 40.

171   With severe heatstroke...death: Mayo Clinic, "Heatstroke," www.mayoclinic.org/diseases-conditions/heat-stroke/symptoms-causes/syc-20353581.

172   Earth is warming faster...years: Chelsea Harvey, "Earth Hasn't Warmed This Fast in Tens of Millions of Years," *Scientific American*, September 13, 2020, www.scientificamerican.com/article/earth-hasnt-warmed-this-fast-in-tens-of-millions-of-years.

172   Currently in the US, heat waves kill...weather: NOAA, "Weather Related Fatality and Injury Statistics," www.weather.gov/hazstat.

172   Approximately 12,000 Americans...causes: Drew Shindell et al., "The Effects of Heat Exposure on Human Mortality throughout the United States," *GeoHealth* 4, no. 4 (April 2020), www.ncbi.nlm.nih.gov/pmc/articles/PMC7125937.

172   Deadly heat waves affect...75 percent: Stephen Leahy, "By 2100, Deadly Heat May Threaten Majority of Humankind," *National Geographic*, July 19, 2017, www.nationalgeographic.com/science/article/heatwaves-climate-change-global-warming.

172   in August 2020...54°C: Concepción de León and John Schwartz, "Death Valley Just Recorded the Hottest Temperature on Earth," *New York Times*, December 7, 2020, www.nytimes.com/2020/08/17/climate/death-valley-hottest-temperature-on-earth.html.

172   Plants and animals are going extinct: Brad Plumer, "Humans Are Speeding Extinction and Altering the Natural World at an 'Unprecedented' Pace," *New York Times*, May 6, 2019, www.nytimes.com/2019/05/06/climate/biodiversity-extinction-united-nations.html.

173   African elephants need thirty to fifty gallons: African Wildlife Foundation, "Elephant," www.awf.org/wildlife-conservation/elephant.

173   Less than 4,000...ago: "Tiger Numbers Show Increase for First Time in a Century," *BBC*, April 11, 2016, www.bbc.com/news/world-asia-36012338.

173   For the Sundarbans tigers...homeless: Kai Schultz and Hari Kumar, "Bengal Tigers May Not Survive Climate Change," *New York Times*, May 6, 2019, www.nytimes.com/2019/05/06/science/tigers-climate-change-sundarbans.html.

174   At a 2°C temperature rise...land on Earth: Jeff Tollefson, "Humans Are Driving One Million Species to Extinction," *Nature*, May 6, 2019, www.nature.com/articles/d41586-019-01448-4.

174   Since 1500, at least 680...extinct: Plumer, "Humans Are Speeding Extinction."

174   Only 3 percent of vertebrate life...animals: Will Steffen, "The Anthropocene: Where on Earth Are We Going?," *Ecological Citizen* 2, no. 2 (July 2018):129–30, www.ecologicalcitizen.net/article.php?t=anthropocene-where-earth-we-going.

174   But as the temperature warms...bite zone: "Climate Change Will Expose Half of World's Population to Disease-Spreading Mosquitoes by 2050," *Yale Environment 360*, March 5, 2019, https://e360.yale.edu/digest/climate-change-will-expose-half-of-worlds-population-to-disease-spreading-mosquitoes-by-2050.

175   As Earth has warmed...geographically: C. Bouchard et al., "N Increased Risk of Tick-Borne Diseases with Climate and Environmental Changes," *Canada Communicable Disease Report* 45, no. 4 (April 2019): 83–89, www.ncbi.nlm.nih.gov/pmc/articles/PMC6587693.

175   The mosquito is the world's deadliest animal: Lydia Ramsey, "These Are the Top 15 Deadliest Animals on Earth," *ScienceAlert*, February 23, 2018, www.sciencealert.com/what-are-the-worlds-15-deadliest-animals.

175   *Aedes aegypti*, a mosquito...midcentury: Joshua Sokol, "The Worst Animal in the World," *The Atlantic*, August 20, 2020, www.theatlantic.com/health/archive/2020/08/how-aedes-aegypti-mosquito-took-over-world/615328.

175   About 300,000 Americans...Lyme disease: Centers for Disease Control and Prevention, "How Many People Get Lyme Disease?," January 13, 2021, www.cdc.gov/lyme/stats/humancases.html.

176   By 2050, 143 million...Latin America: Wallace-Wells, *Uninhabitable Earth*, page 133.

176   By 2100, 13 million...worst hit: Wallace-Wells, *Uninhabitable Earth*, page 131.

176   1.5°C vs. 2°C: IPCC, *Special Report*.

177   Globally, 2020...on record: Andrea Thompson, "NASA Says 2020 Tied for Hottest Year on Record," *Scientific American*, January 14, 2021, www.scientificamerican.com/article/2020-will-rival-2016-for-hottest-year-on-record/.

177   Globally, the 2010s...on record: World Meteorological Organization, "2020 Was One of Three Warmest Years on Record," January 15, 2021, https://public.wmo.int/en/media/press-release/2020-was-one-of-three-warmest-years-record.

CHAPTER 15

179   an average American contributes 14.8 tons...per person: Hannah Ritchie and Max Roser, "Greenhouse Gas Emissions," Our World in Data, https://ourworldindata.org/greenhouse-gas-emissions.

179   Humans need to collectively...2020s: Brady Dennis, "In Bleak Report, U.N. Says Drastic Action Is Only Way to Avoid Worst Effects of Climate Change," *Washington Post*, November 26, 2019, www.washingtonpost.com/climate-environment/2019/11/26/bleak-report-un-says-drastic-action-is-only-way-avoidworst-impacts-climate-change.

179   residential buildings contribute...emissions: Hannah Ritchie and Max Roser, "Emissions by Sector," Our World in Data, https://ourworldindata.org/emissions-by-sector.

180   making and destroying of plastics…plants: Center for International Environmental Law, "Sweeping New Report on Global Environmental Impact of Plastics Reveals Severe Damage to Climate," May 15, 2019, www.ciel.org/news/plasticandclimate.

180   plastic use will go up…decades: Giorgia Guglielmi, "In the Next 30 Years, We'll Make Four Times More Plastic Waste Than We Ever Have," *Science*, July 19, 2017, www.sciencemag.org/news/2017/07/next-30-years-we-ll-make-four-times-more-plastic-waste-we-ever-have.

180   Transportation accounts for about 16 percent of emissions: Ritchie and Roser, "Emissions by Sector."

181   In April 2020…30 percent: Jonathan Lambert, "Emissions Dropped during the COVID-19 Pandemic. The Climate Impact Won't Last," *Science News*, August 7, 2020, www.sciencenews.org/article/covid-19-coronavirus-greenhouse-gas-emissions-climate-change.

181   For the year, global CO_2 emissions…driving habits: Jeff Tollefson, "COVID Curbed Carbon Emissions in 2020—but Not by Much," *Nature*, January 15, 2021, www.nature.com/articles/d41586-021-00090-3.

181   New York to London dumps about .33 metric tons: International Civil Aviation Organization, "ICAO Carbon Emissions Calculator," www.icao.int/environmental-protection/CarbonOffset/Pages/default.aspx.

182   1 billion cattle and that number's growing: Rob Cook, "World Cattle Inventory by Country," Beef Market Central, June 10, 2021, www.beefmarketcentral.com/story-world-cattle-inventory-country-usda-146-106898.

182   Grazing animals contribute…atmosphere: Food and Agriculture Organization of the United Nations, "Major Cuts of Greenhouse Gas Emissions from Livestock within Reach," September 26, 2013, http://www.fao.org/news/story/en/item/197608/icode.

182   Each time we eat a serving of beef…at .07 pounds: Jonathan Safran Foer, *We Are the Weather: Saving the Planet Begins at Breakfast* (Farrar, Straus and Giroux, 2019), page 100.

183   Green energy can create new jobs: Jeff Berardelli, "As Fossil Fuel Jobs Falter, Renewables Come to the Rescue," *CBS News*, September 25, 2020, www.cbsnews.com/news/renewable-energy-jobs-replacing-fossil-fuel-jobs-oil-wind.

185   National Academies of Sciences…geoengineering: Christopher Flavelle, "Should We Block the Sun? Scientists Say the Time Has Come to Study It," *New York Times*, March 25, 2021, www.nytimes.com/2021/03/25/climate/geoengineering-sunlight.html.

185   adding red seaweed to cows' feed: Jennifer Walter, "Feeding Seaweed to Cows Could Curb Their Methane-Laden Burps," *Discover Magazine*, February 10, 2020, www.discovermagazine.com/environment/feeding-seaweed-to-cows-could-curb-their-methane-laden-burps.

186   One plant in Iceland uses giant fans: "Experimental Air Capture Technology in Iceland Aims to Combat Climate Change," *NBC News*, April 19, 2021, www.nbcnews.com/now/video/experimental-air-capture-technology-in-iceland-aims-to-combat-climate-change-110485061723.

186   the US emitted 4.5 billion metric tons: Statista, "Carbon Dioxide Emissions from Energy Consumption in the United States from 1975 to 2020," April 21, 2021, www.statista.com/statistics/183943/us-carbon-dioxide-emissions-from-1999.

187   A more established technology is carbon capture storage: Vincent Gonzales, Alan Krupnick, and Lauren Dunlap, "Carbon Capture and Storage 101," Resources for the Future, May 6, 2020, www.rff.org/publications/explainers /carbon-capture-and-storage-101.

187   In 2020, America's only carbon capture...expensive: Nichola Groom, "Problems Plagued U.S. CO2 Capture Project before Shutdown: Document," *Reuters*, August 6, 2020, www.reuters.com/article/us-usa-energy-carbon-capture /problems-plagued-u-s-co2-capture-project-before-shutdown-document -idUSKCN2523K8.

188   The goal is net-zero carbon emissions by 2050: Glenn Kessler, "Kerry's Claim That 'We Have Nine Years Left' to Avert the Climate Crisis," *Washington Post*, February 22, 2021, www.washingtonpost.com/politics/2021/02/22 /kerrys-claim-that-we-have-nine-years-left-avert-climate-crisis.

188   scientists hesitate to give an exact date: Kessler, "Kerry's Claim."

INDEX

Page numbers in *italics* refer to illustrations in the text.

Cora McAnulty

STACY McANULTY

doesn't think the world will end suddenly, but she does worry about the ongoing damage to the environment caused by her species. Nonetheless, she believes *Homo sapiens* can overcome challenges and reverse course by taking action. Before becoming an author, Stacy was a mechanical engineer (and before that—like in fourth grade—she was an aspiring astronaut). Her love of math and science is reflected in most of her books. She writes chapter books, middle-grade novels, including *The Miscalculations of Lightning Girl*, and picture books, including the Our Universe series, which explores space and the natural world. Originally from New York, she now lives in North Carolina with her family.